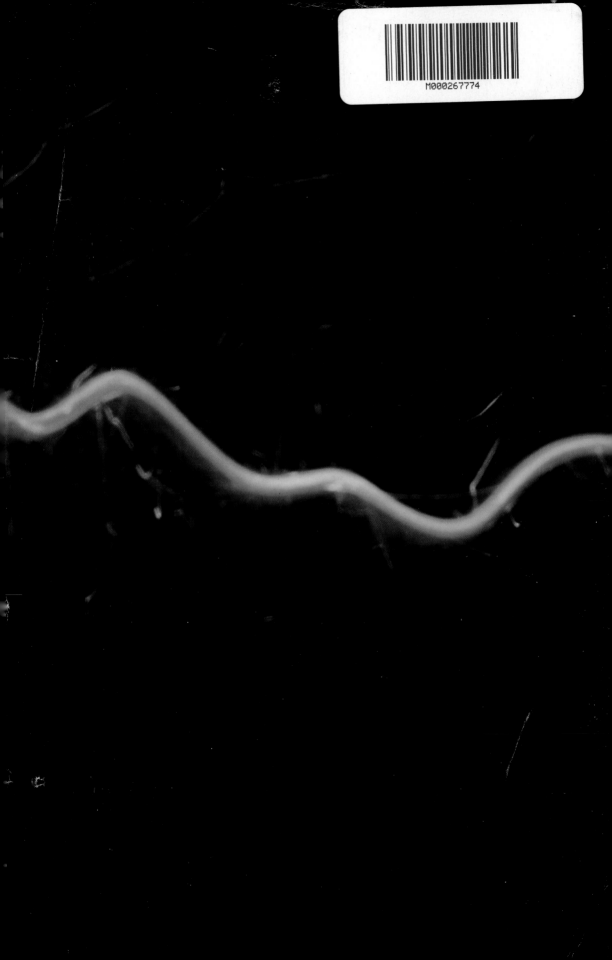

MORE
electric
BREAD®

Innovative Cooking Enterprises

I.C.E., Inc. Anchorage, Alaska ®

Developed by:
INNOVATIVE COOKING ENTERPRISES * I.C.E., INC.

Cover, Book Design & Photography by:
ART & INTERNATIONAL PRODUCTIONS
SASHA SAGAN & JIM TILLY

Written by:
SUZAN NIGHTINGALE

ELECTRIC BREAD® is a registered trademark of
Innovative Cooking Enterprises * I.C.E., Inc.

Published by Innovative Cooking Enterprises * I.C.E., Inc.
            P. O. Box 240888
            Anchorage, Alaska 99524-0888

SAN 297-441X

First Printing September, 1995.
Printed in China

Library of Congress Catalog Card Number: 95-79184

ISBN 0-9629831-6-0

Table of Contents

MORE! MORE!

By popular demand, a whole new world of recipes from the *ELECTRIC BREAD*® team.

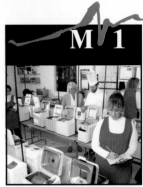

ONLY BY MACHINE

Gourmet recipes at the push of a button

ROLLED AND PULLED

Cut, folded and filled - specialty breads to shape and bake in your conventional oven

EXTRAS

Dough techniques, the latest on accessories, and some extra surprises

M 1
O 1
R 1
E 1

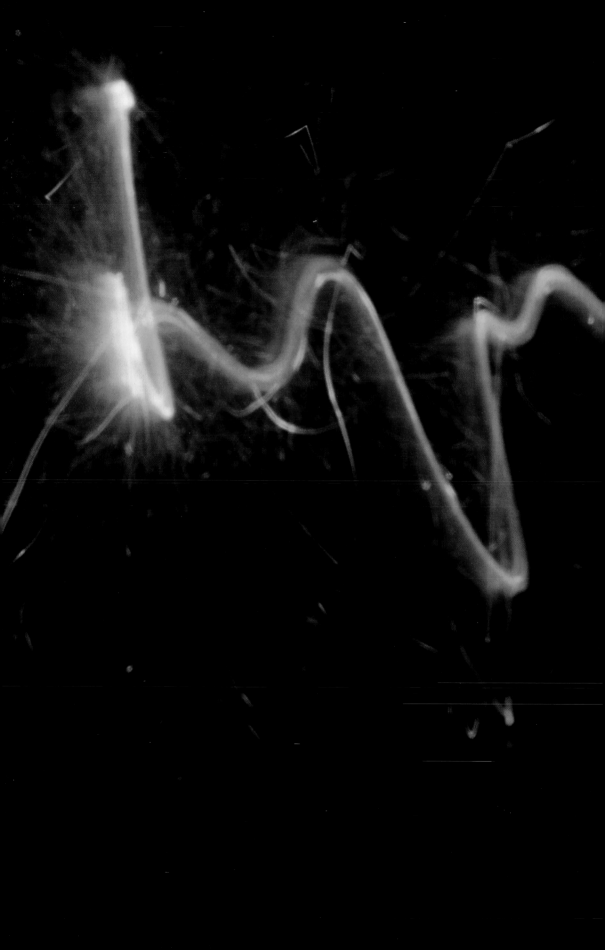

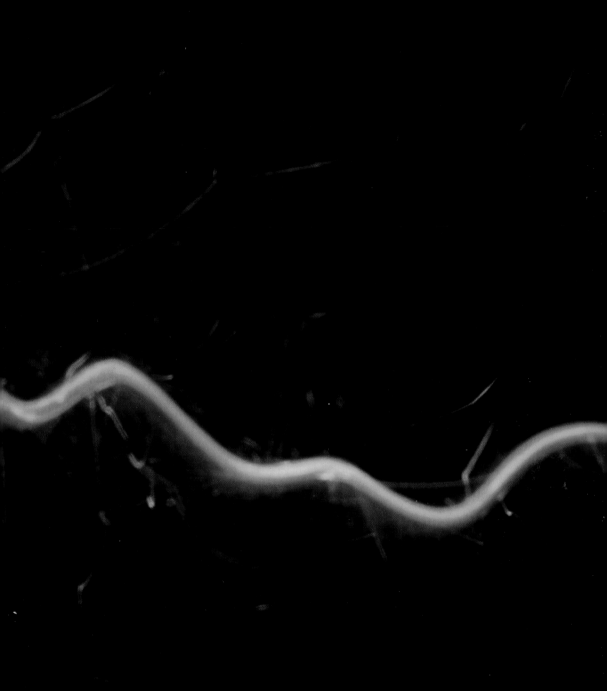

MORE! MORE!

By popular demand, a whole new world of recipes
from the ELECTRIC BREAD® team

Once upon a time - more than 16,000 loaves ago, in fact - we opened the only full-time bread machine test kitchen in the world. We were sure these marvelous machines could produce quality bread every time *with the right recipes*.

Electric Bread® became an industry phenomenon. Still the only bread machine recipe book with a toll-free number – (800) 541-2733 – we get calls daily asking about flour and yeast, ingredients and machine models. And because we talk to home bakers every day, we know what you want.

The secret of our success – the I.C.E. Test Kitchen works with new bread machines, flour and yeast to ensure **Electric Bread**® *recipes work for you.*

"More!" tops the list - more exciting recipes, more innovative baking ideas, more ways to maximize your machine. Well, we heard you!

More Electric Bread® takes you beyond the basics with all new recipes and even more specialty doughs:

* *ONLY IN THE MACHINE* contains classic gourmet breads like Homestyle White and Creamy Rye, plus exciting new flavors like Very Berry and Spicy Beef. There's even a new take on Irish Soda Bread with golden raisins.

* *ROLLED AND PULLED* delivers basic recipes and techniques for bagels, focaccia and rolls - and then goes a step beyond into a wide array of variations for each recipe.

* In *EXTRAS*, you'll find dough techniques to show you how to roll, fold and form any bread machine dough into easy and elegant shapes.

The world of baking has changed since bread machines were introduced a few short years ago. Today's machine owner is ready to experiment, savoring gourmet taste and ease of preparation while enjoying the creativity of new and different presentations. And today's flours and yeasts – some formulated especially for bread machines – make the job easier than ever.

No one has baked more bread in more machines than we have.

Now, with *More Electric Bread*, these proven recipes are yours to bake at home. Enjoy!

OUR RECIPES HAVE BEEN TESTED IN THESE MACHINES:

American Harvest • Betty Crocker • Black & Decker • Breadman • Chefmate
Charlescraft • Circulair • Citizen • Dak • Decosonic • Goldstar • Hitachi
Kenmore • Magic Mill • Mister Loaf • Mr Coffee • National • Oster
Panasonic • Pillsbury • Regal • Salton-Maxim • Sanyo • Singer • Sunbeam
Toastmaster • Welbilt • West Bend • Williams-Sonoma • Zojirushi & others...

Quick Reminders

Recipe Size

The recipe size for you depends on your machine. Different bread machines have different pan capacities. Electric Bread recipes give ingredients for a regular and a large loaf. With a liquid measuring cup, determine how many cups of water your pan holds when filled to the rim. Then use the tested recipe size shown below for your pan capacity.

Pan Capacity	Recipe Size
Less than 12 cups	Regular
12 to 16 cups	Large
More than 16 cups	Double Regular

Measuring

Bread machines don't ask much of the home baker, but they do require one thing: precision. Careful measurements can make the difference between a luscious loaf and a disappointing dud. Our recipes give two yeast measurements – one for <u>fast rise</u> and one for <u>active dry</u>. Be sure to use only the amount for your particular yeast.

Extra Knead

We developed the "extra knead" technique to give bread structure, and to make French bread, whole wheat and pumpernickel. Simply start your machine and let it go through the first knead, then stop and restart it from the beginning again. Some models feature a whole wheat, whole grain or French cycle. These cycles may replace the double knead used in some of our recipes.

FRUIT

Always drain canned fruits to keep an accurate liquid/flour ratio. When using dried fruit, remember that older fruit has a more concentrated sugar content; too much may overactivate the yeast. Beware of fruit (such as apricots) treated with sulfur dioxide; this preservative can kill the yeast. Recipes with a lot of sugar will be darker. For lighter crust use the light setting.

SPOILAGE

Store yeast in a cool, dry, airtight container. Once opened, all yeast should be stored in the refrigerator. Never use perishable ingredients - milk, yogurt, meat, cheese, eggs in a delayed time bake cycle. They can spoil before the baking process even starts.

LOADING YOUR MACHINE

Load ingredients in the order suggested in your owner's manual. For consistency's sake, all of our recipes are listed with the yeast last. For the best results, use our recipes with your own machine's procedures. Keep an eye on the dough during initial mixing. If dough looks too dry or too moist, add water or flour a teaspoon at a time, until ball forms.

WATER TEMPERATURE

Use tepid water in your machine, cold water won't activate the yeast, hot water will speed it too much and very hot water will kill it.

EGGS

Because egg has a dramatic effect on bread texture our recipes call for beaten egg to ensure the correct egg amount. Eggs vary in size, but a typical large egg yields about 3 Tablespoons of beaten egg. Egg Beaters or other real egg substitutes may also be used for beaten eggs.

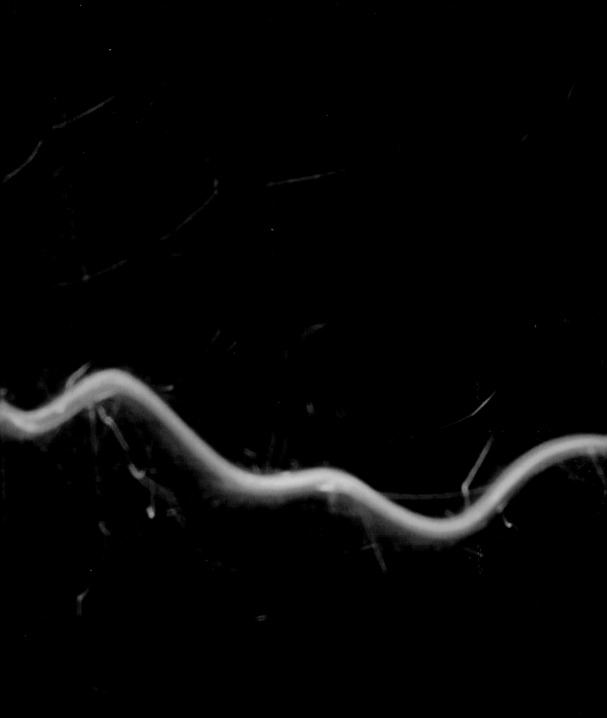

ONLY BY MACHINE

Gourmet recipes at the push of a button

Cinnamon Sunrise

Calories 217   Protein 11 %
Cholesterol 8 mg.   Carbohydrates 59 %
Sodium 240 mg.   Fat 30 %

Nutritional information per serving

Fresh from the oven, this bread explodes with cinnamon flavor as eye-opening as its namesake. Savor it warm and this aromatic loaf will become a classic at your breakfast table. Dress it up as French Toast and you'll never go back to the plain stuff again.

regular loaf		large loaf
3/4 cup	**Water** *lukewarm*	1 1/8 cups
2 1/4 cups	**White Bread Flour**	3 1/3 cups
1 Tbsp.	**Dry Milk**	1 1/2 Tbsp.
2 1/2 Tbsp.	**Brown Sugar**	3 Tbsp.
3/4 tsp.	**Salt**	1 tsp.
2 Tbsp.	**Butter**	1/4 cup
1 1/2 tsp.	**Cinnamon**	2 tsp.
1/3 cup	**Pecan Bits**	1/2 cup
1 tsp.	**Yeast** *fast rise*	1 1/2 tsp.
	- or -	
1 1/4 tsp.	**Yeast** *active dry*	2 tsp.

Success Hints

■ Great served warm for breakfast! Start on a time bake the night before.

■ For the fullest flavor use fresh cinnamon. Fresh spice enhances this bread dramatically.

■ This recipe can be made using the regular, rapid and delayed time bake cycles.

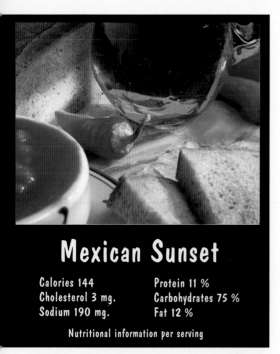

Mexican Sunset

Calories 144   Protein 11 %
Cholesterol 3 mg.   Carbohydrates 75 %
Sodium 190 mg.   Fat 12 %

Nutritional information per serving

This piquant bread brings a South of the Border flavor to any meal. Chunky salsa, fresh cilantro and sour cream marry into a robust flavor that can turn a simple bowl of tomato soup into a whole new company meal. Your tastebuds will shout, "Ole!" Your guests will shout, "More!"

regular loaf		large loaf
1/2 cup	**Water** *lukewarm*	3/4 cup
2 1/4 cups	**White Bread Flour**	3 1/3 cups
1 Tbsp.	**Sugar**	1 1/2 Tbsp.
1/2 tsp.	**Salt**	1 tsp.
1 1/2 Tbsp.	**Taco Mix**	2 1/2 Tbsp.
2 Tbsp.	**Chunky Salsa**	3 Tbsp.
1/4 cup	**Sour Cream**	1/2 cup
1/2 Tbsp.	**Cilantro** *dried* - or -	1 Tbsp.
2 Tbsp.	**Cilantro** *chopped fresh leaves*	3 Tbsp.
3/4 tsp.	**Yeast** *fast rise* - or -	1 1/2 tsp.
3/4 tsp.	**Yeast** *active dry*	1 1/2 tsp.

Success Hints

■ For best flavor, use fresh cilantro.

■ Always use thick, chunky salsa.

■ Dried taco seasoning mix is sold in packets, usually located near gravy mixes.

■ Drain any thin, watery liquid from salsa before using.

■ This recipe can be made using the regular and rapid bake cycles.

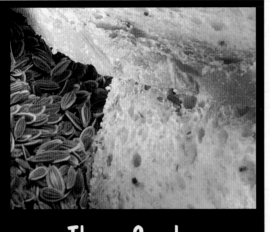

Three Seeds

Calories 182   Protein 13 %
Cholesterol 8 mg.   Carbohydrates 68 %
Sodium 308 mg.   Fat 19 %

Nutritional information per serving

regular loaf		large loaf
3/4 cup	**Water** *lukewarm*	1 1/8 cups
2 1/4 cups	**White Bread Flour**	3 1/3 cups
1 Tbsp.	**Dry Milk**	2 Tbsp.
1 Tbsp.	**Sugar**	1 1/2 Tbsp.
1 tsp.	**Salt**	1 1/2 tsp.
2 Tbsp.	**Butter**	3 Tbsp.
1 tsp.	**Dill Seed**	1 3/4 tsp.
1 tsp.	**Celery Seed**	1 3/4 tsp.
1 tsp.	**Caraway Seed**	1 3/4 tsp.
3/4 tsp.	**Yeast** *fast rise*	1 1/2 tsp.
	- or -	
3/4 tsp.	**Yeast** *active dry*	1 3/4 tsp.

This refreshing bread surprises the palate with its delicate combination of flavors. Equal portions of caraway, celery and dill seeds make this light loaf interesting without overpowering it. Even kids love this lightly seasoned "bug bread." Your cheese sandwiches will never be the same again.

Success Hints

■ Stack seeds on top of other dry ingredients, away from water.

■ This bread makes flavorful stuffing for poultry or pork.

■ Thinly sliced, toasted points make a welcome Sunday Brunch accompaniment to Bloody Marys.

■ This recipe can be made using the regular, rapid and delayed time bake cycles.

Very Berry

Calories 190   Protein 13 %
Cholesterol 4 mg.   Carbohydrates 75 %
Sodium 289 mg.   Fat 12 %

Nutritional information per serving

Reminiscent of a berry pie, this colorful loaf is a party bread that will make your taste buds think *they're* having the party. Imagine strawberries in January, blueberries in February - this favorite dessert bread will keep a taste of summer in your kitchen all year long.

regular loaf		large loaf
3/4 cup	**Water** *lukewarm*	1 1/8 cup
2 1/4 cups	**White Bread Flour**	3 1/4 cups
1/2 Tbsp.	**Dry Milk**	1 Tbsp.
1 Tbsp.	**Brown Sugar**	1 1/2 Tbsp.
1 tsp.	**Salt**	1 1/2 tsp.
1 Tbsp.	**Butter**	2 Tbsp.
1/4 cup	**Rolled Oats** *old fashioned*	1/2 cup
1 1/2 tsp.	**Pure Vanilla**	2 tsp.
1 1/2 Tbsp.	**Raspberry Syrup**	2 Tbsp.
1/2 cup	**Berry Medley** *dried*	3/4 cup
1 tsp.	**Yeast** *fast rise*	1 1/2 tsp.
	- or -	
1 1/2 tsp.	**Yeast** *active dry*	2 tsp.

Success Hints

- We used "Berry Medley" dried fruit mix with strawberries, blueberries and cranberries. (Available in our Accessories Section.)

- Fruit syrups made for flavoring coffee drinks work best. Feel free to experiment with flavors; blueberry can be substituted for raspberry.

- Use old fashioned rolled oats, not instant.

- This recipe can be made using the regular, rapid and delayed time bake cycles. Stack dried fruit away from liquid for delayed time bake.

Espresso

Calories 163
Cholesterol 5 mg.
Sodium 275 mg.

Protein 12 %
Carbohydrates 77 %
Fat 11 %

Nutritional information per serving

regular loaf		large loaf
1/2 cup	**Water** *lukewarm*	3/4 cup
2 cups	**White Bread Flour**	3 1/4 cups
3 Tbsp.	**Sugar**	1/4 cup
1 tsp.	**Salt**	1 1/2 tsp.
2 Tbsp.	**Heavy Cream**	1/4 cup
2 Tbsp.	**Instant Espresso**	3 Tbsp.
2 tsp.	**Pure Vanilla** *extract*	1 Tbsp.
2 Tbsp.	**Yogurt** *vanilla/fat free*	1/4 cup
7/8 tsp.	**Yeast** *fast rise*	1 3/4 tsp.
	- or -	
1 1/4 tsp.	**Yeast** *active dry*	1 3/4 tsp.

It may not take the place of your first cup of Java in the morning, but this coffee-flavored bread is a great way to start the day. Think of it as a latte you can eat with your fingers - and best of all, no spills on the dashboard!

Success Hints

■ Coffee flavored yogurt may be substituted for vanilla yogurt for extra flavor.

■ This dough may look slightly flat - not as round and firm as normal. It will bake up just fine.

■ Leftover bread would make a great bread pudding.

■ This recipe may be made using regular and rapid cycles.

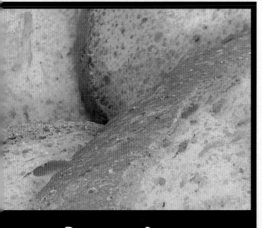

Pepper Corn

Calories 176	Protein 13 %
Cholesterol 4 mg.	Carbohydrates 75 %
Sodium 293 mg.	Fat 12 %

Nutritional information per serving

This isn't your grandma's corn bread. It's lighter than standard corn bread, with a zing that will leave your taste buds gossiping for minutes. Try it with chowders for a hearty supper or use it to redefine the basic roast beef sandwich.

Success Hints

- We like the flavor produced using Lawry's® Seasoned Pepper. It contains a colorful coarse blend of black and red peppers and other spices.

- Use fresh pepper for dramatically more flavor.

- Make your own bread crumbs from this loaf for delicious pan-fried fish.

- Cube leftovers for tasty Caesar Salad croutons.

- This recipe can be made using the regular, rapid and delayed time bake cycles.

regular loaf		large loaf
3/4 cup	**Water** *lukewarm*	1 1/8 cups
2 1/4 cups	**White Bread Flour**	3 1/3 cups
1 Tbsp.	**Dry Milk**	2 Tbsp.
1 Tbsp.	**Sugar**	1 1/2 Tbsp.
1 tsp.	**Salt**	1 1/2 tsp.
1 Tbsp.	**Butter**	2 Tbsp.
1 1/4 tsp.	**Pepper** *seasoned*	2 tsp.
3 Tbsp.	**Cornmeal**	1/3 cup
3/4 tsp.	**Yeast** *fast rise*	1 1/2 tsp.
	- or -	
1 tsp.	**Yeast** *active dry*	1 3/4 tsp.

Irish Soda

Calories 178
Cholesterol 5 mg.
Sodium 315 mg.
Protein 12 %
Carbohydrates 76 %
Fat 12 %

Nutritional information per serving

regular loaf		large loaf
3/4 cup	**Water** *lukewarm*	1 1/8 cup
2 cups	**White Bread Flour**	3 cups
1/2 Tbsp.	**Sugar**	1 Tbsp.
1 tsp.	**Salt**	1 1/2 tsp.
1 Tbsp.	**Butter**	2 Tbsp.
1 1/2 Tbsp.	**Buttermilk** *dried*	2 Tbsp.
1/8 tsp.	**Baking Soda**	1/4 tsp.
1/2 Tbsp.	**Caraway Seeds**	1 Tbsp.
1/2 cup	**Raisins** *golden*	1 cup
1 tsp.	**Yeast** *fast rise*	1 1/2 tsp.
	- or -	
1 1/2 tsp.	**Yeast** *active dry*	2 tsp.

Just the thing with an afternoon "cuppa," our version of traditional Irish Soda Bread combines the sweetness of raisins and richness of caraway with the lightness of a bread. The result is an inviting loaf equally at home in soft slices on the tea table or fresh from the toaster for a winning breakfast.

Success Hints

■ Golden raisins give this bread its light flavor and look. Dark raisins may be substituted but will make a darker, slightly heavier loaf.

■ The sugar in the raisins creates a darker crust; use your machine's "light crust setting" if it has one.

■ Dried buttermilk can generally be found in the baking goods section of your supermarket. If you can't find buttermilk, regular dried milk can be substituted.

■ If using delayed time bake, place raisins atop dry ingredients away from liquid.

■ This recipe can be made using the regular, rapid and delayed time bake cycles.

Millet

Calories 216
Cholesterol 0 mg.
Sodium 140 mg.

Protein 13 %
Carbohydrates 71 %
Fat 16 %

Nutritional information per serving

regular loaf		large loaf
3/4 cup	**Water** *lukewarm*	1 1/4 cup
1 cup	**White Bread Flour**	1 1/2 cups
1 cup	**Wheat Bread Flour**	1 1/2 cups
1 Tbsp.	**Dry Milk**	1 1/2 Tbsp.
1 1/2 Tbsp.	**Sugar**	2 Tbsp.
1/2 tsp.	**Salt**	3/4 tsp.
1 Tbsp.	**Vegetable Oil**	1 1/2 Tbsp.
1/3 cup	**Millet**	1/2 cup
2 Tbsp.	**Flax Seed**	2 1/2 Tbsp.
1 1/2 tsp.	**Yeast** *fast rise*	2 1/4 tsp.
	- or -	
2 1/4 tsp.	**Yeast** *active dry*	3 tsp.

There's an unmistakable crunch in every bite of this chewy loaf. The healthful fiber will stick to your ribs *and* gladden your heart. Enjoy this bread as hearty morning toast with jam, or as a tuna sandwich that will carry you through until supper.

Success Hints

■ Millet and flax seeds can be found in the nutritional and natural food sections of your grocery store.

■ Denture wearers may want to exercise a little caution before biting into this crunchy loaf.

■ Top with Honey Butter from the Spreads section of *Electric Bread*® for a morning treat.

■ This recipe can be made using the regular, rapid and delayed time bake cycles.

French Wheat

Calories 141   Protein 13 %
Cholesterol 4 mg.   Carbohydrates 73 %
Sodium 287 mg.   Fat 14 %

Nutritional information per serving

regular loaf		large loaf
3/4 cup	**Water** *lukewarm*	1 1/8 cup
1 3/4 cups	**White Bread Flour**	2 1/2 cups
1/4 cup	**Wheat Bread Flour**	1/2 cups
1 1/2 tsp.	**Sugar**	2 1/4 tsp.
1 tsp.	**Salt**	1 1/2 tsp.
1 Tbsp.	**Butter**	1 1/2 Tbsp.
1 1/2 tsp.	**Yeast** *fast rise*	2 tsp.
	- or -	
1 1/2 tsp.	**Yeast** *active dry*	3 tsp.

Ooh, la,la! A simple recipe for simply wonderful bread. This versatile, slightly shorter, loaf goes with anything – beef, pasta, chicken, fish – but stands alone with a simple pat of butter, too. This one is bound to become a repeat visitor to your dinner table.

Success Hints

- To develop the crisp crust that French bread is known for, use your French cycle. If your machine doesn't have a French cycle, simply start your machine and let it go through the first knead, then stop and restart it from the beginning again. This gives the bread extra kneading time and results in a crisp crust.

- Because of the distinctive chewy French crust, we recommend serving this bread within 24 hours to avoid toughness.

- For traditional French baguettes, shape this dough using the French baguette technique on page E-6.

- This recipe can be made using the regular, rapid and delayed time bake cycles.

Olive

Calories 194
Cholesterol 3 mg.
Sodium 409 mg.

Protein 13 %
Carbohydrates 65 %
Fat 22 %

Nutritional information per serving

One bite of this rich loaf and you'll be transported to a sunny piazza in the Mediterranean. The olive oil marries with black and green olives for a moist texture that lasts and lasts. Serve this versatile bread with a roast leg of lamb – or make your own pizza crust and stand back for compliments.

regular loaf		large loaf
1/2 cup	**Water** *lukewarm*	3/4 cup
2 1/3 cups	**White Bread Flour**	3 1/2 cups
1 Tbsp.	**Dry Milk**	2 Tbsp.
1/2 Tbsp.	**Sugar**	1 Tbsp.
3/4 tsp.	**Salt**	1 1/4 tsp.
1 Tbsp.	**Olive Oil**	2 Tbsp
1/4 cup	**Green Olives** *whole stuffed*	1/2 cup
1/2 cup	**Black Olives** *whole pitted*	3/4 cup
3 Tbsp.	**Blue Cheese** *crumbled*	1/4 cup
1 tsp.	**Yeast** *fast rise*	1 1/2 tsp.
	- or -	
1 1/2 tsp.	**Yeast** *active dry*	2 tsp.

Success Hints

- Drain olives well in a colander, then shake well to remove any excess liquid.

- Pitted and stuffed olives can be added whole. Kneading will break them into pieces.

- Feta cheese makes a zesty topping when this dough is used for pizza crust.

- This recipe can be made with regular or rapid bake cycles.

Maple Walnut

Calories 176   Protein 14 %
Cholesterol 2 mg.   Carbohydrates 64 %
Sodium 283 mg.   Fat 22 %

Nutritional information per serving

This bread starts smelling good as soon as you measure the ingredients, and it just gets better from there. Think of French Toast slathered in syrup, and you'll have the essence of this sweet breakfast bread. Pop it in the toaster and your feast awaits.

Success Hints

- Mapleine can be substituted equally for maple extract.

- If clove flavor is too pronounced, diminish amount, according to your taste.

- Top this bread with pineapple cream cheese and we promise your taste buds will start a conga line!

- This recipe can be made using the regular, rapid and delayed time bake cycles.

regular loaf		large loaf
3/4 cup	**Water** *lukewarm*	1 1/8 cup
1 1/2 cups	**White Bread Flour**	2 1/2 cups
1/2 cup	**Wheat Bread Flour**	1/2 cup
1 Tbsp.	**Dry Milk**	1 1/2 Tbsp.
1 tsp.	**Salt**	1 1/2 tsp.
1/2 Tbsp.	**Butter**	1 Tbsp.
1 Tbsp.	**Maple Syrup**	1 1/2 Tbsp.
1 1/2 Tbsp.	**Brown Sugar**	1 3/4 Tbsp.
1/3 cup	**Walnuts** *chopped*	1/2 cup
1 tsp.	**Maple Extract**	1 1/2 tsp.
1/4 tsp.	**Cloves** *chopped*	1/2 tsp.
1 1/8 tsp.	**Yeast** *fast rise*	1 3/4 tsp.
	- or -	
1 1/2 tsp.	**Yeast** *active dry*	2 1/2 tsp.

Kugelhopf

Calories 207   Protein 13 %
Cholesterol 6 mg.   Carbohydrates 61 %
Sodium 231 mg.   Fat 26 %

Nutritional information per serving

This sweet Alsatian bread is usually served as a Name Day cake, eaten on the birthday of one's patron saint. Traditionally baked in a fluted pan topped with almonds, this delicately sweet loaf is a festive addition to any meal. You can serve it right out of your machine or transfer kneaded dough to a bundt pan for a traditional presentation.

Success Hints

- To serve traditionally, transfer kneaded dough after first rise to a buttered bundt or ring mold. Sprinkle slivered almonds into pan before placing dough in, and then top dough with more almonds. Allow to rise about one hour and then bake at 375° for 40 – 50 minutes. Immediately remove from pan.

- This recipe can be made using regular and rapid bake cycles.

regular loaf		large loaf
3/4 cup	**Water** *lukewarm*	1 cup
2 cups	**White Bread Flour**	3 cups
1 Tbsp.	**Dry Milk**	1 1/2 Tbsp.
2 Tbsp.	**Sugar**	3 Tbsp.
3/4 tsp.	**Salt**	1 tsp.
1 1/2 Tbsp.	**Butter**	2 Tbsp.
1 tsp.	**Lemon Zest** *fresh*	1 3/4 tsp.
1/4 cup	**Almonds** *chopped*	1/3 cup
1/4 cup	**Raisins** *Golden*	1/3 cup
1/2 tsp.	**Vanilla Extract**	3/4 tsp.
1 tsp.	**Yeast** *fast rise*	2 tsp.
	- or -	
1 3/4 tsp.	**Yeast** *active dry*	3 tsp.

Tomato Basil

Calories 152   Protein 13 %
Cholesterol 0 mg.   Carbohydrates 71 %
Sodium 283 mg.   Fat 16 %

Nutritional information per serving

regular loaf		large loaf
3/4 cup	**Water** *lukewarm*	1 1/8 cup
2 cups	**White Bread Flour**	3 cups
1 1/2 Tbsp.	**Dry Milk**	2 Tbsp.
1 tsp.	**Sugar**	1 1/2 tsp.
1 tsp.	**Salt**	2 tsp.
1 Tbsp.	**Olive Oil**	2 Tbsp.
1 1/2 Tbsp.	**Tomato Paste**	2 Tbsp.
1 Tbsp.	**Italian Seasoning**	1 1/2 Tbsp.
1 1/2 tsp.	**Minced Garlic**	2 tsp.
3/4 tsp.	**Yeast** *fast rise*	2 tsp.
	- or -	
1 1/4 tsp.	**Yeast** *active dry*	3 tsp.

This sunset-colored bread comple-
ments any Italian dish, and makes a
hot meatball sandwich something to
write home about. Save a couple of
slices for dynamite croutons, too.

Success Hints

- For fuller flavor, heat garlic in olive
  oil for 30 seconds in your micro-
  wave and cool before adding.

- Minced garlic can be purchased in
  a jar. In our market, it's kept next
  to the fresh garlic in the produce
  section.

- Garlic paste can be substituted in
  equal amounts for minced garlic.

- Italian Seasoning may be found in
  the Italian foods section or the
  spices section of your market.

- This recipe can be made using
  regular and rapid bake cycles.

Garlic Blues

Calories 165
Cholesterol 2 mg.
Sodium 305 mg.

Protein 13 %
Carbohydrates 68 %
Fat 19 %

Nutritional information per serving

regular loaf		large loaf
3/4 cup	**Water** *lukewarm*	1 1/8 cups
2 cups + 2 Tbsp.	**White Bread Flour**	3 cups
1 Tbsp.	**Dry Milk**	1 1/2 Tbsp.
2 tsp.	**Sugar**	3 tsp.
1 tsp.	**Salt**	1 1/2 tsp.
1 tsp.	**Vegetable Oil**	1 1/2 tsp.
1 Tbsp.	**Garlic** *paste*	1 1/2 Tbsp.
1/8 cup	**Blue Cheese** *crumbled*	1/4 cup
1 tsp.	**Yeast** *fast rise*	1 1/2 tsp.
	- or -	
3/4 tsp.	**Yeast** *active dry*	1 1/4 tsp.

Oh, ah woke up this mornin' and made me some bread... As improvisational as the blues themselves, this subtle loaf features great garlic flavor with just a bite of blue cheese. Its even, light texture makes it a welcome accompaniment for creamy chowder or your favorite salad.

Success Hints

- When measuring blue cheese, do not pack solid. Fill measuring cup with crumbled cheese, packing lightly.

- Although the blue cheese jazzes up this recipe, it may create a wavier crust than other loaves.

- Minced garlic can be substituted in equal amounts for gourmet garlic paste.

- This recipe can be made using the regular and rapid bake cycles.

Rice Pudding

Calories 190   Protein 11 %
Cholesterol 5 mg.   Carbohydrates 73 %
Sodium 279 mg.   Fat 16 %

Nutritional information per serving

Our chef, Tim, created this comforting loaf using simple, every day ingredients. It's a perfect way to use leftover rice, but you'll love this subtle, sweet loaf so much, we bet you don't wait for leftovers to make it again.

regular loaf		large loaf
1/3 cup	**Water** *lukewarm*	2/3 cup
2 cups	**White Bread Flour**	3 cups
1/2 cup	**Cooked White Rice**	2/3 cup
1/2 cup.	**Sour Cream**	3/4 cup
1 1/2 Tbsp.	**Brown Sugar**	2 Tbsp.
1 tsp.	**Salt**	1 1/2 tsp.
1/4 tsp.	**Allspice**	1/2 tsp.
1 tsp.	**Cinnamon**	1 1/2 tsp.
1/3 cup	**Raisins**	1/2 cup
1 tsp.	**Vanilla**	1 1/2 tsp.
1 1/4 tsp.	**Yeast** *fast rise*	2 tsp.
	- or -	
2 tsp.	**Yeast** *active dry*	3 tsp.

Success Hints

■ Let cooked rice cool before using.

■ Spoon rice lightly into measuring cup without packing.

■ This recipe can be made using regular and rapid bake cycles.

Corn Fritter

Calories 217   Protein 13 %
Cholesterol 15 mg.   Carbohydrates 65 %
Sodium 360 mg.   Fat 27 %

Nutritional information per serving

When Mary Ann served this luscious loaf with ribs, everyone ignored the ribs until the bread was nothing but a honey and butter-coated memory! A slightly sweet alternative to traditional corn bread, this popular loaf makes a colorful accompaniment to chili, too.

Success Hints

■ Be sure to drain canned corn *very* well before measuring.

■ Dough will not be as firm in the kneading process as you're used to. Relax, it will rise to the occasion.

■ To make fried corn fritters, use the dough cycle. Roll dough out into a one-inch thickness and then slice into one-inch cubes. Drop into pre-heated cooking oil (fritters should sizzle immediately) for approximately one minute, stirring occasionally. Remove with a slotted spoon and drain.

regular loaf		large loaf
1/4 cup	**Water** *lukewarm*	1/3 cup
2 cups	**White Bread Flour**	3 cups
2 Tbsp.	**Dry Milk**	3 Tbsp.
1 tsp.	**Salt**	1 1/2 tsp.
3 Tbsp.	**Butter**	1/4 cup
3 Tbsp.	**Honey**	1/4 cup
1/2 cup	**Canned Corn** *drained*	3/4 cup
1 1/2 Tbsp.	**Chives** *dried/chopped*	2 Tbsp.
3 Tbsp.	**Sour Cream**	1/4 cup
1 tsp.	**Yeast** *fast rise*	2 tsp.
	- or -	
1 1/2 tsp.	**Yeast** *active dry*	2 1/2 tsp.

■ This recipe is recommended for regular and rapid bake cycles.

Onion Walnut

Calories 253   Protein 14 %
Cholesterol 0 mg.   Carbohydrates 53 %
Sodium 274 mg.   Fat 33 %

Nutritional information per serving

This is onion bread like you've never had before, dancing with walnuts in every bite. Jonell won cheers from her family when she used this bread to make an Alaska-style tuna melt substituting fresh halibut in an open-faced sandwich.

regular loaf		large loaf
5/8 cup	**Water** *lukewarm*	1 cup
2 cups	**White Bread Flour**	3 cups
1 Tbsp.	**Dry Milk**	2 Tbsp.
1/2 Tbsp.	**Sugar**	1 Tbsp.
1 tsp.	**Salt**	1 1/2 tsp.
1 Tbsp.	**Walnut Oil**	2 Tbsp.
2 Tbsp.	**Cereal** *100% whole wheat*	1/3 cup
1 1/2 Tbsp.	**Toasted Dried Onions**	2 1/2 Tbsp.
1/2 Tbsp.	**Dried Parsley**	1 Tbsp.
3/4 cup	**Walnuts** *coarse chopped*	1 1/4 cups
1 tsp.	**Yeast** *fast rise*	2 tsp.
	- or -	
1 1/2 tsp.	**Yeast** *active dry*	2 1/2 tsp.

Success Hints

■ Toasted onions are sold with spices, or you can make them in your oven. Simply sprinkle chopped dried onions on a cookie sheet and bake at 350° for 3-5 minutes. Stir to ensure even browning, and watch closely to avoid over-browning.

■ Walnuts can also be toasted using above method.

■ Use a 100% whole wheat cooked cereal, not a flaked cold cereal. Measure cereal uncooked directly from the package. We used Zoom® found near the oatmeal in our market.

■ This recipe can be made using the regular, rapid and delayed time bake cycles. If using time delayed cycle, stack dried onions out of liquid.

Spicy Beef

Calories 170	Protein 20 %
Cholesterol 10 mg.	Carbohydrates 65 %
Sodium 518 mg.	Fat 15 %

Nutritional information per serving

Hold on, mama, we're talking *spicy*! This is definitely a grown-up bread with an unmistakable bite. Sliced fresh, it's not a side dish but the star of the main event. Shaped into buns, it makes hamburgers a gourmet experience.

regular loaf		large loaf
1/2 cup + 2 Tbsp.	**Water** *lukewarm*	1 cup
1 2/3 cups	**White Bread Flour**	2 1/2 cups
1/3 cup	**Wheat Bread Flour**	1/2 cup
1 1/2 Tbsp.	**Brown Sugar**	2 Tbsp.
1/2 cup	**Dried Beef** *chopped*	3/4 cup
1 1/2 Tbsp.	**Black Olives** *chopped*	2 Tbsp.
2 tsp.	**Dried Onions**	1 Tbsp.
2 Tbsp.	**Cream Cheese** *softened*	3 Tbsp.
1 1/2 tsp.	**Dried Red Peppers** *crushed*	2 tsp.
3/4 tsp.	**Pepper Corns** *whole green*	1 tsp.
5/8 tsp.	**Yeast** *fast rise*	1 1/2 tsp.
	- or -	
1 1/8 tsp.	**Yeast** *active dry*	2 1/8 tsp.

Success Hints

- Fat-free cream cheese is not recommended for this recipe.

- This dough makes killer croutons - or, slice fingers of bread and brown in garlic butter for an appetizer.

- We use chopped dried onions, but you could substitute minced.

- This recipe can be made using regular and rapid bake cycles.

Thai Bread

Calories 193	Protein 13 %	
Cholesterol 3 mg.	Carbohydrates 58 %	
Sodium 303 mg.	Fat 29 %	

Nutritional information per serving

regular loaf		large loaf
1/2 cup	**Water** *lukewarm*	7/8 cup
2 cups	**White Bread Flour**	3 cups
1 1/2 Tbsp.	**Dry Milk**	2 Tbsp.
1 1/2 Tbsp.	**Sugar**	2 Tbsp.
1 tsp.	**Salt**	1 1/2 tsp.
2 tsp.	**Butter**	1 Tbsp.
1 tsp.	**Chili Paste** *Sambal Oeleck*	1 1/2 tsp.
2 tsp.	**Lime Juice**	1 Tbsp.
1/4 cup	**Peanuts** *unsalted/chopped*	1/3 cup
1/4 cup	**Coconut Milk**	1/3 cup
1 tsp.	**Sesame Seed Oil**	2 tsp.
1/2 tsp.	**Lemon Zest**	3/4 tsp.
2 tsp.	**Cilantro** *dried*	1 Tbsp.
1 tsp.	**Yeast** *fast rise*	2 tsp.
	- or -	
1 1/2 tsp.	**Yeast** *active dry*	2 1/2 tsp.

Put two chefs together, thinking about ordering in some Thai food, and what do you get? Tim and Greg came up with this subtle taste of Thailand while fantasizing about dinner one night. This one is truly unique.

Success Hints

- Always use Sambal Oeleck chili paste, not chili sauce. This paste, sesame oil and coconut milk are usually found in the oriental food section of your grocery store.

- For more punch, use fresh cilantro and double the amount.

- If you like more fire in your Thai food, increase the chili paste in this recipe.

- Always use fresh lemon zest, not dried peel. Lime zest can be substituted for lemon.

- This recipe can be made using regular and rapid bake cycles.

Holiday Cranberry

Calories 165   Protein 13 %
Cholesterol 4 mg.   Carbohydrates 75 %
Sodium 293 mg.   Fat 12 %

Nutritional information per serving

Two words say it all: French Toast.
Or maybe: Turkey Sandwich. Or
was that: Cheese Sandwich? How
about simply: Christmas morning!
Once you've baked this aromatic loaf,
you'll fall into rhapsodies too. This
full-bodied sweet bread is as versatile as it is unexpected. We promise
you won't want to save it just for
special occasions.

Success Hints

■ The fresher your spices the zestier
   this bread will taste.

■ For time-delay bake, place dried
   cranberries and yeast on top of
   flour away from liquids to keep
   them dry until machine starts.

■ Unsweetened bottled lemon juice
   may be used in lieu of freshly
   squeezed juice.

regular loaf		large loaf
3/4 cup	**Water** *lukewarm*	1 1/8 cups
2 cups	**White Bread Flour**	3 cups
1 Tbsp.	**Dry Milk**	1 1/2 Tbsp.
1 1/2 Tbsp.	**Sugar**	2 Tbsp.
1 tsp.	**Salt**	1 1/2 tsp.
1 Tbsp.	**Butter**	2 Tbsp.
1/4 tsp.	**Cloves** *ground*	1/2 tsp.
3/4 tsp.	**Cinnamon**	1 tsp.
1/2 tsp.	**Allspice**	3/4 tsp.
1/2 tsp.	**Orange** *pure extract*	3/4 tsp.
1 tsp.	**Lemon Juice**	2 tsp.
1/2 cup	**Cranberries** *dried*	1 cup
1 tsp.	**Yeast** *fast rise*	2 tsp.
	- or -	
1 1/4 tsp.	**Yeast** *active dry*	2 1/4 tsp.

■ This recipe can be made using the
   regular, rapid and delayed time
   bake cycles.

Wild Rice

Calories 178   Protein 13 %
Cholesterol 6 mg.   Carbohydrates 57 %
Sodium 298 mg.   Fat 30 %

Nutritional information per serving

This light textured bread is packed with good stuff. The rice and oats add a stick-to-your-ribs goodness while the wheat berry lends a distinctive crunch. Serve it with a hearty soup and no one will leave the table hungry.

Success Hints

■ Drain cooked wild rice well before measuring. Cool to room temperature. May also use leftover wild rice.

■ Use uncooked old-fashioned rolled oats, not instant.

■ Wheat berry is sold in bulk at health food stores. Cracked wheat may be substituted, but the crunch will be lost.

■ This recipe can be made using the regular, rapid and delayed time bake cycles.

regular loaf		large loaf
1/2 cup + 2 Tbsp.	**Water** *lukewarm*	1 cup
2 cups	**White Bread Flour**	3 cups
1 Tbsp.	**Dry Milk**	2 Tbsp.
2 Tbsp.	**Brown Sugar**	3 Tbsp.
1 tsp.	**Salt**	1 1/2 tsp.
1 1/2 Tbsp.	**Butter**	2 Tbsp.
1/3 cup	**Cooked Wild Rice**	1/2 cup
1/2 cup	**Rolled Oats**	3/4 cup
2 Tbsp.	**Wheat Berry**	2 1/2 Tbsp.
1 tsp.	**Yeast** *fast rise*	1 1/2 tsp.
	- or -	
1 1/2 tsp.	**Yeast** *active dry*	2 tsp.

Cheezy Ranch

Calories 194   Protein 16 %
Cholesterol 20 mg.   Carbohydrates 65 %
Sodium 330 mg.   Fat 17 %

Nutritional information per serving

regular loaf		large loaf
1/3 cup + 1 Tbsp.	**Water** *lukewarm*	1/2 cup
2 1/4 cups	**White Bread Flour**	3 cups
3/4 Tbsp.	**Sugar**	1 1/2 Tbsp.
3/4 tsp.	**Salt**	1 1/2 tsp.
1 Tbsp.	**Buttermilk** *dried*	2 Tbsp.
1/4 cup	**Yogurt** *plain*	1/2 cup
2 Tbsp.	**Beaten Egg**	3 Tbsp.
2 tsp.	**Dressing** *Ranch/powdered mix*	1 Tbsp.
1/2 cup	**Sharp Cheddar Cheese** *shredded*	3/4 cup
1 tsp.	**Yeast** *fast rise*	2 tsp.
	- or -	
1 1/2 tsp.	**Yeast** *active dry*	2 1/2 tsp.

Jim, our graphic designer and resident humorist, says Cheezy Ranch is his favorite - "to serve to all my cheesy friends." But the only thing cheesy about this loaf is its rich Ranch dressing and cheddar flavor. If you're looking for the bread that will turn a bowl of soup or a salad into a meal, this is it.

Success Hints

- Be sure to use the dried Ranch dressing that comes in packets.

- Use sharp cheddar for the best flavor. Load cheese into measuring cup gently, don't pack solid.

- Use *plain* not vanilla yogurt.

- Even the crust has a flavor all its own; don't let the kids cut if off!

- This recipe can be made using the regular and rapid bake cycles.

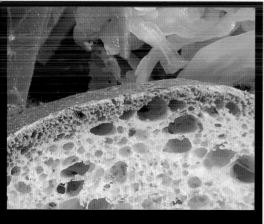

Reuben, Reuben

Calories 216   Protein 19 %
Cholesterol 29 mg.   Carbohydrates 52 %
Sodium 479 mg.   Fat 28 %

Nutritional information per serving

regular loaf		large loaf
1/4 cup	**Water** *lukewarm*	1/2 cup
2 cups	**White Bread Flour**	3 cups
1 Tbsp.	**Sugar**	2 Tbsp.
1 tsp.	**Salt**	1 1/2 tsp.
1 Tbsp.	**Buttermilk** *dried*	2 Tbsp.
1/4 cup	**Plain Yogurt**	1/2 cup
1/2 cup	**Muenster Cheese** *shredded*	3/4 cup
2 Tbsp.	**Beaten Egg**	3 Tbsp.
2 Tbsp.	**Sauerkraut**	3 Tbsp.
1/4 cup	**Pastrami**	1/2 cup
5/8 tsp.	**Yeast** *fast rise*	1 1/2 tsp.
	- or -	
3/4 tsp.	**Yeast** *active dry*	1 3/8 tsp.

Suzan's sons, Martin and Cameron, like company to guess this bread's "secret" ingredient - the sauerkraut is that subtle. Inspired by the classic Reuben, this bread is versatile enough to enhance your favorite deli creation but mild enough to serve with any meal. It has a wonderful, even texture, too.

Success Hints

- Drain sauerkraut before measuring.

- Serve with corned beef and cabbage for a meal made in heaven.

- Dried buttermilk is generally located in the baking goods section of your grocery store. Regular dried milk can be substituted.

- This recipe may be made using regular and rapid bake cycles.

Home Style White

Calories 215
Cholesterol 25 mg.
Sodium 335 mg.

Protein 14 %
Carbohydrates 61 %
Fat 25 %

Nutritional information per serving

regular loaf		large loaf
5/8 cup	**Water** *lukewarm*	1 1/8 cups
2 1/4 cups	**White Bread Flour**	3 1/4 cups
1/4 cup	**Dry Milk**	1/3 cup
1 tsp.	**Salt**	1 1/2 tsp.
3 Tbsp.	**Butter**	1/4 cup
2 Tbsp.	**Honey**	3 Tbsp.
2 Tbsp.	**Beaten Egg**	3 Tbsp.
1/2 tsp.	**Yeast** *fast rise*	1 tsp.
	- or -	
3/4 tsp.	**Yeast** *active dry*	1 1/4 tsp.

This is bread like Grandma used to make, rich and full-bodied enough for dinner rolls or piled-high sandwiches from heaven. The egg adds texture missing in store-bought and helps make this elegant loaf as versatile as it is basic.

Success Hints

- The honey in this recipe makes the loaf prone to a darker crust; use a "light crust" setting when possible.

- This dough makes great dinner rolls. Shape and bake this recipe using any of the Dough Techniques found on pages E-1 through E-6.

- During kneading, dough may appear wet. This is normal.

- This recipe may be made using regular and rapid bake cycles.

Chocolate

Calories 158		Protein 14 %
Cholesterol 9 mg.		Carbohydrates 78 %
Sodium 276 mg.		Fat 8 %

Nutritional information per serving

Chocolate lovers unite! Here's a sweet bread so versatile, our photographer, Sasha, envisioned it as a torte. Other voices say, "No, top it with peanut butter!" "Serve it with ice cream!" Then there's the cream cheese and raspberry jam contingent. There's no wrong way to serve this luscious loaf - all by itself with a glass of milk works just fine, as any kid will tell you.

Success Hints

- Put the chocolate chips into the pan before other ingredients to ensure even melting.

- To make a Mint Chocolate version, substitute mint flavored chips for Semi-Sweet and mint extract for the vanilla.

- This recipe may be made using regular and rapid bake cycles.

regular loaf		large loaf
3/4 cup	**Water** *lukewarm*	1 1/8 cup
2 cups	**White Bread Flour**	3 cups
2 2/3 Tbsp.	**Sugar**	4 Tbsp.
1 tsp.	**Salt**	1 1/2 tsp.
2 2/3 Tbsp.	**Cocoa Powder** *unsweetened*	4 Tbsp.
1/3 cup	**Mini Chocolate Chips** *Semi-Sweet*	1/2 cup
1/4 tsp.	**Vanilla**	1/2 tsp.
2 Tbsp.	**Beaten Egg**	3 Tbsp.
1 tsp.	**Yeast** *fast rise*	1 1/2 tsp.
	- or -	
1 3/4 tsp.	**Yeast** *active dry*	2 1/4 tsp.

Sweet Ho Yin

Calories 179
Cholesterol 3 mg.
Sodium 283 mg.

Protein 12 %
Carbohydrates 68 %
Fat 20 %

Nutritional information per serving

Kids love this sweet bread flavored with Chinese Five Spice, so we named it after the sweetest little Chinese boy we know. Serve it for morning toast and you won't have to beg the kids to eat breakfast anymore. Use it for French Toast and you have the beginnings of a gourmet brunch.

regular loaf		large loaf
3/4 cup	**Water** *lukewarm*	1 1/4 cup
2 cups	**White Bread Flour**	3 cups
3 Tbsp.	**Brown Sugar**	1/4 cup
1 tsp.	**Salt**	1 1/2 tsp.
2 tsp.	**Butter**	1 Tbsp.
1 tsp.	**Chinese Five Spice**	1 1/2 tsp.
1/4 cup	**Cashews** *chopped*	1/3 cup
1 tsp.	**Orange Extract**	1 1/2 tsp.
1 tsp.	**Yeast** *fast rise*	1 1/2 tsp.
	- or -	
1 1/2 tsp.	**Yeast** *active dry*	2 tsp.

Success Hints

■ Add orange extract with water, away from yeast.

■ This is a great "beginner bread" for kids to make. It's deceptively simple and everyone loves it.

■ Top this bread with the sweet Guava-Raisin Spread from *Electric Bread*® for a real dessert treat.

■ This recipe can be made using the regular, rapid and delayed time bake cycles.

Creamy Rye

Calories 184
Cholesterol 9 mg.
Sodium 299 mg.

Protein 11 %
Carbohydrates 68 %
Fat 21 %

Nutritional information per serving

Get out the pastrami and cheese for this superb rye bread. One of the lightest ryes we've tasted, it offers a rich, full flavor that travels easily from the breakfast table to the dinner table. So smooth, we had to call it creamy. This one's definitely a keeper.

regular loaf		large loaf
1/2 cup + 2 Tbsp.	**Water** *lukewarm*	7/8 cup
1 3/4 cups	**White Bread Flour**	2 1/2 cups
1 1/2 tsp.	**Caraway Seeds**	2 tsp.
1 tsp.	**Salt**	1 1/2 tsp.
1 1/2 Tbsp.	**Butter**	2 Tbsp
1 1/2 Tbsp.	**Brown Sugar**	2 Tbsp.
1/2 cup	**Rye Flour**	3/4 cup
1 tsp.	**Cocoa Powder** *unsweetened*	1 1/2 tsp.
1/4 cup	**Sour Cream**	1/2 cup
1 Tbsp.	**Molasses**	1 1/2 Tbsp.
3/4 tsp.	**Yeast** *fast rise*	1 1/8 tsp.
	- or -	
1 1/8 tsp.	**Yeast** *active dry*	2 tsp.

Success Hints

■ For a different kind of snack, top with chutney-cheese spread from *Electric Bread*®.

■ This recipe can be made using regular or rapid rise cycles.

Smoky Almond

Calories 222   Protein 14 %
Cholesterol 4 mg.   Carbohydrates 58 %
Sodium 277 mg.   Fat 28 %

Nutritional information per serving

No, you don't have to set your machine on fire to get this one-of-a-kind flavor. Smoked almonds do the trick for a truly different kind of bread. Slice thin and top with salmon mousse or gravlax for an unexpected hors d'oeuvre. Or form into buns for cook-out burger flavor all year round.

regular loaf		large loaf
3/4 cup	**Water** *lukewarm*	1 1/8 cup
2 1/3 cups	**White Bread Flour**	3 cups
1 1/2 Tbsp.	**Sugar**	2 Tbsp.
3/4 tsp.	**Salt**	1 tsp.
1 Tbsp.	**Butter**	1 1/2 Tbsp
1/2 cup	**Smoked Almonds** *crushed*	3/4 cup
1 tsp.	**Almond Extract**	1 1/2 tsp.
1 tsp.	**Yeast** *fast rise*	1 3/4 tsp.
	- or -	
1 3/4 tsp.	**Yeast** *active dry*	2 1/2 tsp.

Success Hints

- For a more enhanced smoke flavor add 1/4 teaspoon (regular loaf) or 1/2 teaspoon (large loaf) of Liquid Smoke.

- Use pure almond extract to avoid bitterness.

- This recipe can be made using regular and rapid rise cycles.

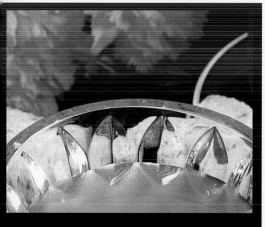

Jodi's Rum Cake

Calories 202   Protein 12 %
Cholesterol 7 mg.   Carbohydrates 59 %
Sodium 305 mg.   Fat 24 %

Nutritional information per serving

regular loaf		large loaf
3/4 cup	**Water** *lukewarm*	1 cup
2 cups	**White Bread Flour**	3 cups
2 Tbsp.	**Dry Milk**	2 1/2 Tbsp.
1/2 tsp.	**Rum Extract**	3/4 tsp.
1 tsp.	**Salt**	1 1/2 tsp.
1 1/2 Tbsp.	**Butter**	2 Tbsp
2 1/2 Tbsp.	**Brown Sugar**	3 Tbsp.
2 1/2 Tbsp.	**Dark Rum**	3 1/2 Tbsp.
1/4 cup	**Pecan Bits**	1/3 cup
1 tsp.	**Yeast** *fast rise*	1 1/2 tsp.
	- or -	
1 3/4 tsp.	**Yeast** *active dry*	2 1/4 tsp.

Lynn was thinking of her mother-in-law's Christmas rum cake when she made this rich holiday bread. Bake several of these sweet loaves and wrap them as gifts – but don't forget the rum bath, a nectar worthy of its own dipping bowl.

Success Hints

- For miniature gifts, prepare this dough using the Mini-Loaves technique on page E-2.

- This recipe can be made using regular and rapid bake cycles.

Rum Bath

1/2 cup	**Sugar**
1/8 cup	**Water**
1/4 cup	**Butter**
1/4 cup	**Dark Rum**

In a sauce pan, bring sugar, butter and water to a boil. Stir three more minutes then add rum, bring back to a boil and remove from heat. With warm bread on rack, poke holes in top of bread using chop stick or similar long, sharp object. Drizzle rum bath down the holes. Or simply cube the loaf and use the rum bath for dunking.

Portuguese Sweet

Calories 216		Protein 12 %
Cholesterol 36 mg.		Carbohydrates 62 %
Sodium 333 mg.		Fat 26 %

Nutritional information per serving

Our college friend, Kate, speaks fondly of a roommate whose mother sent weekly packages of this sweet bread all the way from Guam! Portuguese traders introduced this rich egg bread to the South Pacific a hundred years ago. We first tasted it in Hawaii, and look forward to it on return visits. Try it once, and you will too.

Success Hints

- This recipe produces a soupy-looking dough. As kneading progresses, the potato flakes will absorb the moisture.

- Two words: French Toast

- This bread makes a darker loaf. If available, bake on the light crust setting.

- This recipe can be made using regular and rapid bake cycles.

regular loaf		large loaf
1/2 cup	**Water** *lukewarm*	3/4 cup
2 cups	**White Bread Flour**	3 cups
1 Tbsp.	**Dry Milk**	1 1/2 Tbsp.
1/4 cup	**Sugar**	1/3 cup
1 tsp.	**Salt**	1 1/2 tsp.
2 Tbsp.	**Butter**	3 Tbsp.
1/4 cup	**Beaten Egg**	1/3 cup
1/2 tsp.	**Lemon Zest** *fresh*	3/4 tsp.
3/4 tsp.	**Vanilla Extract** *pure*	1 tsp.
1/4 cup	**Potato Flakes** *dried*	1/3 cup
2 Tbsp.	**Pineapple Concentrate** *frozen (thawed)*	3 Tbsp.
3/4 tsp.	**Yeast** *fast rise*	1 tsp.
	- or -	
1 tsp.	**Yeast** *active dry*	1 1/2 tsp.

Zesty Orange

Calories 220   Protein 13 %
Cholesterol 8 mg.   Carbohydrates 59 %
Sodium 239 mg.   Fat 28 %

Nutritional information per serving

If you're seeking a tangy bread with a real citrus zip, look no more. This is a natural for toast and eggs on those cold winter mornings. Or top it with cream cheese and marmalade for a warm and welcome tea time treat.

regular loaf		large loaf
5/8 cup	**Water** *lukewarm*	1 cup
2 1/4 cups	**White Bread Flour**	3 cups
1 Tbsp.	**Dry Milk**	1 1/2 Tbsp.
2 1/2 Tbsp.	**Sugar**	3 Tbsp.
3/4 tsp.	**Salt**	1 tsp.
2 Tbsp.	**Butter**	3 Tbsp
2 Tbsp.	**Orange Zest** *fresh*	2 1/2 Tbsp.
3/4 tsp.	**Cinnamon**	1 tsp.
2 tsp.	**Orange Extract**	2 1/2 tsp.
1/3 cup	**Pecan Bits**	1/2 cup
1 tsp.	**Yeast** *fast rise*	1 1/2 tsp.
	- or -	
1 1/2 tsp.	**Yeast** *active dry*	2 1/4 tsp.

Success Hints

■ Zest only the bright orange part of the peel; zesting the white under-peel can result in bitterness.

■ Try topping with Orange Honey Butter from the *Electric Bread*® Sweet and Savory Spreads section.

■ This recipe can be made using the regular and rapid bake cycle.

Whole Wheat Spice

Calories 161
Cholesterol 6 mg.
Sodium 165 mg.

Protein 13 %
Carbohydrates 70 %
Fat 17 %

Nutritional information per serving

You'll enjoy the goodness of whole wheat and the tingle of spices in this aromatic loaf. Sergei envisioned this bread as an elegant breakfast, served with roses and apple juice in a hand-cut glass over 100 years old.

Success Hints

- Top with Simple Chutney Cheese spread from *Electric Bread*® and serve with apple slices. Mmmm.

- This recipe can be made using the regular, rapid and delayed time bake cycles.

regular loaf		large loaf
3/4 cup	**Water** lukewarm	1 1/4 cup
1 cup	**White Bread Flour**	1 1/2 cups
1 cup	**Wheat Bread Flour**	1 1/2 cups
1 Tbsp.	**Dry Milk**	1 1/2 Tbsp.
1 1/2 Tbsp.	**Brown Sugar**	2 Tbsp.
1/2 tsp.	**Salt**	3/4 tsp.
1 1/2 Tbsp.	**Butter**	2 Tbsp.
1/4 cup	**Raisins**	1/2 cup
1 tsp.	**Vanilla**	1 1/2 tsp.
3/4 tsp.	**Cinnamon**	1 tsp.
1/4 tsp.	**Nutmeg**	1/2 tsp.
1/4 tsp.	**Ginger** ground	1/2 tsp.
1 1/4 tsp.	**Yeast** fast rise	1 5/8 tsp.
	- or -	
2 1/8 tsp.	**Yeast** active dry	2 1/2 tsp.

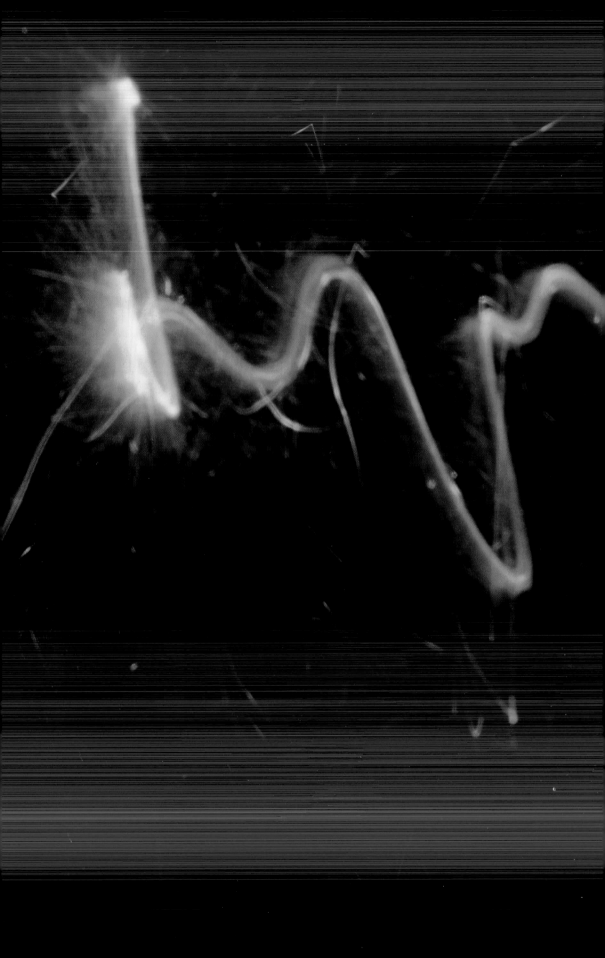

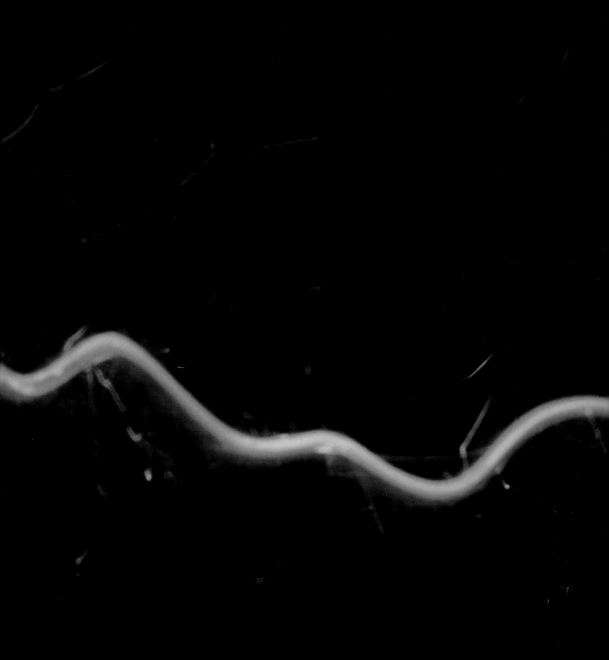

ROLLED AND PULLED

Cut, folded and filled — specialty breads
to shape and bake in your conventional oven

Basic Bagel

Calories 352	Protein 13 %
Cholesterol 12 mg.	Carbohydrates 80 %
Sodium 191 mg.	Fat 5 %

Nutritional information per serving

regular loaf		large loaf
3/4 cup	**Water** *lukewarm*	1 1/8 cup
2 cups	**White Bread Flour**	3 cups
2 Tbsp.	**Brown Sugar**	3 1/3 Tbsp.
3/4 tsp.	**Salt**	1 tsp.
1 1/2 tsp.	**Yeast** *fast rise*	2 1/2 tsp.
	- or -	
2 1/4 tsp.	**Yeast** *active dry*	3 1/4 tsp.

Is there anything as simple - and as versatile - as a bagel? No longer the exclusive domain of the big city deli, bagels are as likely to be found at the lunch table as the breakfast counter. Now you can turn this simple, sweet dough into moist, chewy bagels that stay fresh for days.

Remove dough from the machine after the first knead - aproximately 20 to 30 minutes.

EGG WASH
1 egg and 1 Tbsp. water

Success Hints

- See page R-3 for hints on making the best of bagels.

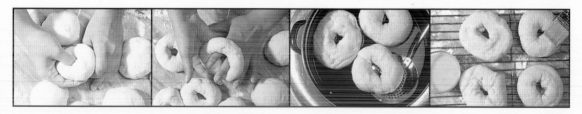

Place dough on floured surface. Divide into 8 parts for a large loaf and 5 parts for a regular. Form balls, gently press thumb through center of ball and slowly stretch into bagel shape. While bagels rise, bring 3 quarts water and 1 Tbsp. sugar to a rapid boil in a large sauce pan. Drop test dough (see hint on R-3). Using a slotted spoon, drop 2-3 bagels into rapidly boiling water. Boil on each side for 1 1/2 minutes. Remove and cool on rack 1 minute, brush with egg and sprinkle with sesame or poppy seeds, if desired. Bake at 400° on a baking sheet sprinkled with cornmeal, until golden – approx. 15 minutes.

and even More Bagels

• When forming bagels, set aside two 1/4" balls of dough. When bagels have doubled in size, drop the test dough into boiling water. Dough should pop to the top right away. When this happens, it is time to boil the bagels.

• A quick spray of non-stick vegetable coating on the top of the bagel may be substituted for the egg wash.

• To make Bagel Sticks, cut bagel before rising and lay out in a straight line. Roll sticks in a combination of sesame and poppy seeds with a pinch of garlic powder. Let sticks rise, boil, and bake as described in Basic Bagel process steps on R-1.

• To make Bagel Chips, slice leftover bagels horizontally into thin slices. Brush with butter or margarine on one side. Lay (butter side up) on ungreased cookie sheet and bake at 325° for 12-15 minutes until golden brown and crisp

Whole Wheat Bagels

These whole wheat bagels will rise to meet your expectations. Try adding 1 Tbsp. of flax or sunflower seeds for a heartier bagel and don't forget to try sprinkling seeds on top of bagels as well.

regular		large
3/4 cup	**Water** *lukewarm*	1 1/8 cups
1 1/4 cups	**White Bread Flour**	2 cups
3/4 cup	**Wheat Bread Flour**	1 cup
2 Tbsp.	**Brown Sugar**	3 1/3 Tbsp.
1 1/3 Tbsp.	**Gluten**	2 Tbsp.
3/4 tsp.	**Salt**	1 tsp.
1 1/2 tsp.	**Yeast** *fast rise*	2 1/2 tsp.
	-or-	
2 1/4 tsp.	**Yeast** *active dry*	3 1/4 tsp.

Place all ingredients in machine and prepare dough using Basic Bagel process steps on page R-1.

Pumpkin Spice Bagels

Pumpkin, spice, and everything nice is what you'll find in these bagels. We love them toasted for breakfast on a cool fall morning.

regular		large
1/4 cup + 1 Tbsp.	**Water** lukewarm	1/2 cup +2 Tbsp.
2 cups	**White Bread Flour**	3 cups
4 Tbsp.	**Brown Sugar**	6 Tbsp.
3/4 tsp.	**Salt**	1 tsp.
1/3 cup	**Pumpkin** canned	1/2 cup
1 tsp.	**Cinnamon**	1 1/2 tsp.
1/4 tsp.	**Ground Cloves**	1/3 tsp.
1 tsp.	**Nutmeg**	1 1/2 tsp.
1/2 tsp.	**Allspice**	3/4 tsp.
1 1/2 tsp.	**Yeast** fast rise	2 1/2 tsp.
	-or-	
2 1/4 tsp.	**Yeast** active dry	3 1/4 tsp.

Place all ingredients in machine and prepare dough using Basic Bagel process steps on page R-1. (Be sure to use unsweetened canned pumpkin, not pumpkin pie mix.) For incredible bagel chips, sprinkle cinnamon sugar on top of bagel slices before baking.

Cheese Bagels

More please! This is the response these bagels will receive. The cheese-filled centers make them everyone's favorite.

regular		large
2/3 cup	**Grated Cheese** Cheddar/Jack/other	1 cup
3/4 cup	**Water** lukewarm	1 1/8 cups
2 cups	**White Bread Flour**	3 cups
2 Tbsp.	**Brown Sugar**	3 1/3 Tbsp.
3/4 tsp.	**Salt**	1 tsp.
1 1/2 tsp.	**Yeast** fast rise	2 1/2 tsp.
	-or-	
2 1/4 tsp.	**Yeast** active dry	3 1/4 tsp.

Place half of the cheese and all other ingredients into the machine. Reserve the other half of the cheese for sprinkling on bagels after boiling.

Start machine and prepare dough using the Basic Bagel process steps on page R-1.

For Bacon & Cheese Bagels, add 4 Tbsp. of real bacon bits to the cheese. Experiment with different kinds of cheese - Jalapeno, Jack, Colby and Cheddar. Remember, filling the bagel centers with cheese adds lots of flavor. These bagels make wonderful bagel chips.

and even More Bagels

Onion Bagels

Topped with toasted onions, these bagels are superb for sandwiches. Try turning them into bagel chips for an afternoon snack.

Presoak 1/4 cup of dried onions in 1/3 cup warm water for 10 minutes. Drain and press water from onions. Place other ingredients into machine, including the amount of presoaked onions shown. Reserve excess presoaked onions for sprinkling on top of bagels.

Start machine and prepare dough using Basic Bagel process steps on page R-1. (Sometimes the onions retain too much moisture. If dough is too wet, add extra flour a teaspoon at a time until ball forms.)

regular		large
3/4 cup	**Water** *lukewarm*	1 1/8 cups
2 cups + 2 tsp.	**White Bread Flour**	3 cups + 1 Tbsp.
2 Tbsp.	**Brown Sugar**	3 1/3 Tbsp.
3/4 tsp.	**Salt**	1 tsp.
1/2 tsp.	**Onion Powder**	3/4 tsp.
1 tsp.	**Dried Onions** *presoaked*	1 1/2 tsp.
1 1/2 tsp.	**Yeast** *fast rise*	2 1/2 tsp.
	-or-	
2 1/4 tsp.	**Yeast** *active dry*	3 1/4 tsp.

Cinnamon Raisin Bagels

Hot from the oven or toasted, these bagels get great reviews. For a flavor change, soak the raisins in your favorite sweet liquor instead of water.

Soak the raisins in warm water for 10 minutes. Drain and pat dry. Toss with cinnamon and sugar, then place in machine with other ingredients.

Start machine and prepare dough using Basic Bagel process steps on page R-1. Try with the cinnamon sugar bagel topping on page E-7 of our Accessory Section.

regular		large
1/3 cup	**Raisins** *presoaked*	1/2 cup
2 tsp.	**Cinnamon**	1 Tbsp.
2 tsp.	**Sugar**	1 Tbsp.
3/4 cup	**Water** *lukewarm*	1 1/8 cups
2 cups	**White Bread Flour**	3 cups
2 Tbsp.	**Brown Sugar**	3 1/3 Tbsp.
3/4 tsp.	**Salt**	1 tsp.
1 1/2 tsp.	**Yeast** *fast rise*	2 1/2 tsp.
	-or-	
2 1/4 tsp.	**Yeast** *active dry*	3 1/4 tsp.

Cranberry Orange Bagels

A turkey sandwich on this bagel will create Thanksgiving any time of year!

Place all ingredients in machine and prepare dough using the Basic Bagel process steps on page R-1. (Remember to grate only the orange part of the peel - the white part is bitter.)

Serve toasted with orange-honey butter on page 143 of *Electric Bread®*.

If you can't find dried cranberries in your area, try Chukar brand dried fruits from our Accessory Section.

regular		large
3/4 cup	**Water** *lukewarm*	1 1/8 cups
2 cups	**White Bread Flour**	3 cups
3 Tbsp.	**Brown Sugar**	5 Tbsp.
3/4 tsp.	**Salt**	1 tsp.
1/3 cup	**Cranberries** *dried*	1/2 cup
1/4 tsp.	**Cloves** *ground*	1/3 tsp.
1 Tbsp.	**Orange Zest** *fresh/grated*	1 1/2 Tbsp.
1 1/2 tsp.	**Yeast** *fast rise*	2 1/2 tsp.
	-or-	
2 1/4 tsp.	**Yeast** *active dry*	3 1/4 tsp.

Garlic Bagels

Trying to convert someone to bagels? Then this is the bagel for you. Form the bagel as a bagel stick (see Sucess Hints) and serve them warm with spaghetti. Bagels have never looked so good for dinner!

Place all ingredients into machine and prepare dough using Basic Bagel process steps on page R-1. Sprinkle with garlic bread seasoning after boiling or try using the spiced cheese topping in our Focaccia Toppings on page E-7 of our Accessory Section.

regular		large
3/4 cup	**Water** *lukewarm*	1 1/8 cups
2 cups + 2 tsp.	**White Bread Flour**	3 cups + 1 Tbsp.
2 Tbsp.	**Brown Sugar**	3 1/3 Tbsp.
3/4 tsp.	**Salt**	1 tsp.
1/2 tsp.	**Garlic Powder**	3/4 tsp.
1/3 tsp.	**Minced Garlic** *processed*	1/2 tsp.
1 1/2 tsp.	**Yeast** *fast rise*	2 1/2 tsp.
	-or-	
2 1/4 tsp.	**Yeast** *active dry*	3 1/4 tsp.

Basic Focaccia

Calories 219		Protein 8 %
Cholesterol 0 mg.		Carbohydrates 47 %
Sodium 203 mg.		Fat 45 %

Nutritional information per serving

regular loaf		large loaf
3/4 cup	**Water** *lukewarm*	1 1/4 cup
2 cups	**White Bread Flour**	3 1/2 cups
3/4 tsp.	**Salt**	1 tsp.
3 Tbsp.	**Olive Oil**	1/3 cup
3/4 tsp.	**Yeast** *fast rise*	1 1/2 tsp.
	- or -	
1 1/4 tsp.	**Yeast** *active dry*	1 3/4 tsp.

Remove dough from machine after dough cycle is complete or before baking begins on machines without dough cycles.

How could anything so exotic be so easy? This Italian bread is the perfect change of pace when you want something truly different. Simply turn out the dough in a pan and sprinkle with the toppings of your choice. Sweet or savory - *mangiata*!

Success Hints

- See Page R-9 for hints on making super focaccia.

- When available substitute fresh herbs by tripling dried herb measurement.

GARLIC-HERB TOPPING

3 Tbsp.	**Olive Oil**	5 Tbsp.
1/2 tsp.	**Dried Oregano**	3/4 tsp.
1 tsp.	**Dried Rosemary**	1 1/2 tsp.
1 tsp.	**Minced Garlic**	1 1/2 tsp.

Saute oil, oregano and rosemary over medium heat for about 5 minutes while dough is rising. then add garlic and set aside to cool. Pour on dough, add fresh ground pepper to taste and bake.

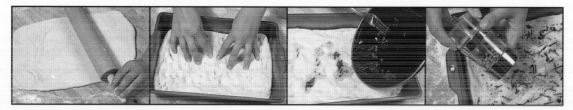

Roll dough on a floured surface into a 10" x 16" rectangle for a large loaf and 9" x 13" for a regular. Place dough into a baking pan or sheet greased with olive oil and dimple with fingers. Let rise 45 minutes until almost doubled in size and gently re-dimple dough. Cover dough with topping ingredients in same order listed in the recipe, pooling olive oil in dimples. Sprinkle with fresh ground pepper to taste. Bake at 400° for 15 to 20 minutes until edges are golden brown.

and even More Focaccia

Success Hints

- Try making individual focaccia, 8 for a large loaf and 5 for a regular. See Tomato & Onion Focaccia photo on next page.

- Give your focaccia more flavor by adding to the dough of the predominant herb or cheese topping of the focaccia (2 tsp. for a large and 1 tsp. for a regular).

- Experiment. Put focaccia in different shape pans or create a different shape on the baking sheet. The important thing is to make the dough into a 1/4" thickness before rise.

- If you live in a dry climate, cover the focaccia during rising with a piece of plastic wrap sprayed with nonstick vegetable spray.

- You can substitute your favorite herbs, vegetables or fruits. Use the Basic Dough for herbs and vegetables and the Sweet Dough for fruits and nuts. Just pour the olive oil on the dough, and then add the topping of your choice.

- For quick and easy focaccia, use the dough and olive oil shown in these recipes in combination with the focaccia toppings in our Accessory Section on page E-7.

Sun Dried Tomato Focaccia

Basic Dough

regular		large
3/4 cup	**Water** *lukewarm*	1 1/4 cups
2 cups	**White Bread Flour**	3 1/2 cups
3/4 tsp.	**Salt**	1 tsp.
2 Tbsp.	**Olive Oil**	3 1/3 Tbsp.
1/3 cup	**Sun Dried Tomatoes** *packed in oil*	1/2 cup
1/2 tsp.	**Minced Garlic** *processed*	3/4 tsp.
1 Tbsp.	**Dried Sweet Basil**	1 1/3 Tbsp.
3/4 tsp.	**Yeast** *fast rise*	1 1/2 tsp.
	-or-	
1 1/4 tsp.	**Yeast** *active dry*	1 3/4 tsp.

Topping

regular		large
2 Tbsp.	**Olive Oil**	3 1/2 Tbsp.
2 Tbsp.	**Fresh Parmesan** *grated*	3 Tbsp.
2 Tbsp.	**Fresh Romano** *grated*	3 Tbsp.
2 tsp.	**Dried Basil**	1 Tbsp.
1 tsp.	**Garlic Powder**	1 1/2 tsp.
1 tsp.	**Italian Seasoning**	1 1/2 tsp.
	Fresh Ground Pepper to Taste	

Drain oil from sun-dried tomatoes and place with other ingredients in machine. Prepare focaccia as shown in Focaccia process steps on page R-7.

Tomato & Onion Focaccia

Basic Dough

regular		large
3/4 cup	**Water** *lukewarm*	1 1/4 cups
2 cups	**White Bread Flour**	3 1/2 cups
3/4 tsp.	**Salt**	1 tsp.
3 Tbsp.	**Olive Oil**	1/3 cup
3/4 tsp.	**Yeast** *fast rise*	1 1/2 tsp.
	-or-	
1 1/4 tsp.	**Yeast** *active dry*	1 3/4 tsp.

Topping

regular		large
3 Tbsp.	**Olive Oil**	5 Tbsp.
1/2 cup	**White Onions** *fresh/chopped*	3/4 cup
1 cup	**Tomatoes** *stewed*	1 1/2 cup
2 Tbsp.	**Black Olives** *sliced*	3 Tbsp.
1/4 tsp.	**Garlic Powder**	1/2 tsp.
	Fresh Ground Pepper to Taste	

Place dough ingredients in machine, start, and process as described on R-7. While dough is in machine, slowly saute onions in 2 Tbsp. of olive oil for about 8 minutes. Add tomatoes and saute over medium heat until the *excess* liquid is gone. Set aside to cool. After dimpling dough, spread with remaining olive oil and tomato mixture. Set dough to rise. After rise, sprinkle with olives, garlic powder and pepper. (Fresh grated parmesan is a nice addition or try substituting anchovies for the olives.)

Sweet Pepper Focaccia

Basic Dough

regular		large
3/4 cup	**Water** *lukewarm*	1 1/4 cups
2 cups	**White Bread Flour**	3 1/2 cups
3/4 tsp.	**Salt**	1 tsp.
3 Tbsp.	**Olive Oil**	1/3 cup
3/4 tsp.	**Yeast** *fast rise*	1 1/2 tsp.
	-or-	
1 1/4 tsp.	**Yeast** *active dry*	1 3/4 tsp.

Topping

regular		large
3 Tbsp.	**Olive Oil**	5 Tbsp.
1/3 cup	**Red Pepper** *fresh/sliced*	1/2 cup
1/3 cup	**Yellow Pepper** *fresh/sliced*	1/2 cup
1/4 cup	**Mushrooms** *fresh/sliced*	1/3 cup
	Fresh Ground Pepper to Taste	

Place dough ingredients in machine, start, and process as described on R-7. While dough is rising, saute peppers and mushrooms in olive oil over medium heat until soft. Set aside to cool. Follow remaining process steps on page R-7.

and even More Focaccia

Simple Focaccia

Basic Dough

regular		large
3/4 cup	**Water** *lukewarm*	1 1/4 cups
2 cups	**White Bread Flour**	3 1/2 cups
3/4 tsp.	**Salt**	1 tsp.
3 Tbsp.	**Olive Oil**	1/3 cup
3/4 tsp.	**Yeast** *fast rise*	1 1/2 tsp.
	-or-	
1 1/4 tsp.	**Yeast** *active dry*	1 3/4 tsp.

Topping

regular		large
2 Tbsp.	**Olive Oil**	3 Tbsp.

Fresh Ground Pepper to Taste

Place dough ingredients in machine, start, and process as described on R-7. This is the focaccia we like to use as the base for the prepackaged focaccia sprinkles available in our Accessory section on page E-7. Simple, easy and with great flavor!

Rosemary Cheese Focaccia

Basic Dough

regular		large
3/4 cup	**Water** *lukewarm*	1 1/4 cups
2 cups	**White Bread Flour**	3 1/2 cups
3/4 tsp.	**Salt**	1 tsp.
3 Tbsp.	**Olive Oil**	1/3 cup
3/4 tsp.	**Yeast** *fast rise*	1 1/2 tsp.
	-or-	
1 1/4 tsp.	**Yeast** *active dry*	1 3/4 tsp.

Topping

regular		large
2 Tbsp.	**Olive Oil**	3 1/2 Tbsp.
2 Tbsp.	**Fresh Parmesan** *grated*	3 Tbsp.
2 Tbsp.	**Fresh Romano** *grated*	3 Tbsp.
2 tsp.	**Rosemary** *dried*	1 Tbsp.

Place dough ingredients in machine, start, and process as described on R-7. We like to use this focaccia as a substitute for garlic bread. You may also sprinkle a little garlic powder on top to make a great garlic cheese focaccia.

Apple Focaccia

Sweet Dough

regular		large
3/4 cup	**Water** *lukewarm*	1 1/4 cups
2 cups	**White Bread Flour**	3 1/2 cups
3/4 tsp.	**Salt**	1 tsp.
2 Tbsp.	**Olive Oil**	1/4 cup
2 Tbsp.	**Sugar**	3 Tbsp.
3/4 tsp.	**Yeast** *fast rise*	1 1/4 tsp.
-or-		
1 1/4 tsp.	**Yeast** *active dry*	1 3/4 tsp.

Place dough ingredients in machine, start, and process as described on page R-7. While dough is rising, toss the apples in the cinnamon and sugar. After rise, arrange apples on top of dough and drizzle with olive oil.

Topping

regular		large
1 cup	**Green Apples** *thinly sliced/unpeeled*	1 1/2 cups
1 cup	**Red Apples** *thinly sliced/unpeeled*	1 1/2 cups
1/2 Tbsp.	**Cinnamon**	1 Tbsp.
2 Tbsp.	**Sugar**	3 Tbsp.
2 Tbsp.	**Olive Oil**	3 1/2 Tbsp.

Ambrosia Focaccia

Sweet Dough

regular		large
3/4 cup	**Water** *lukewarm*	1 1/4 cups
2 cups	**White Bread Flour**	3 1/2 cups
3/4 tsp.	**Salt**	1 tsp.
2 Tbsp.	**Olive Oil**	1/4 cup
2 Tbsp.	**Sugar**	3 Tbsp.
3/4 tsp.	**Yeast** *fast rise*	1 1/4 tsp.
-or-		
1 1/4 tsp.	**Yeast** *active dry*	1 3/4 tsp.

Place dough ingredients in machine, start, and process as described on page R-7. For a totally different orange flavor, use fresh oranges with raisins and walnuts tossed in cinnamon as the topping ingredients.

Topping

regular		large
2 Tbsp.	**Olive Oil**	3 1/2 Tbsp.
12	**Pineapple Rings** *canned slices/drained*	16
3/4 cup	**Mandarin Oranges** *canned/drained*	1 cup
1/4 cup	**Coconut** *shredded*	1/3 cup
1 tsp.	**Cinnamon**	2 tsp.

Basic Cinnamon Roll

Calories 276	Protein 11 %
Cholesterol 21 mg.	Carbohydrates 54 %
Sodium 87 mg.	Fat 35 %

Nutritional information per serving

regular		large
3/4 cup	**Water** *lukewarm*	1 1/8 cup
2 cups	**White Bread Flour**	3 cups
1 1/2 Tbsp.	**Dry Milk**	2 Tbsp.
2 1/3 Tbsp.	**Sugar**	3 1/2 Tbsp.
1/2 tsp.	**Salt**	1 tsp.
2 Tbsp.	**Butter**	3 Tbsp.
1 tsp.	**Yeast** *fast rise*	2 tsp.
	- or -	
2 tsp.	**Yeast** *active dry*	3 tsp.

Is there anything like kicking back with warm sweet rolls and the Sunday paper to know the weekend has finally arrived? Our favorite newlywed, Lara, already has started a Sunday tradition at her house - these succulent cinnamon rolls. Try them once and you'll become a traditionalist, too.

Filling		
3 Tbsp.	**Butter**	1/4 cup
1/3 cup	**Sugar**	1/2 cup
2 tsp.	**Cinnamon**	1 Tbsp.
1/3 cup	**Raisins**	1/2 cup
1/4 cup	**Walnuts**	1/3 cup

Success Hints

- See page R-15 for hints on making great sweet rolls.

Turn out dough onto a floured surface. Roll into 10" x 12" rectangle for a large loaf and 10" x 10" for a regular. Spread butter over dough followed by other "wet" ingredients, then sprinkle sugar and other "dry" ingredients over dough. Roll dough up lengthwise and seal edge by pinching dough together. Slice into 1" pieces, 12 for a large and 8 for a regular. Place in greased pan 1" apart, and let rise until double in size, about 1 hour. Bake at 375° for 15-20 minutes.

and even More Sweet Rolls

Basic Sweet Roll Dough

Use this recipe to make the dough for your sweet rolls, then add the filling of your choice. Place ingredients in machine and then process dough using Basic Cinnamon Roll steps on page R-13.

regular		large
3/4 cup	**Water** *lukewarm*	1 1/8 cups
2 cups	**White Bread Flour**	3 cups
1 1/2 Tbsp.	**Dry Milk**	2 Tbsp.
2 1/3 Tbsp.	**Sugar**	3 1/2 Tbsp.
1/2 tsp.	**Salt**	1 tsp.
2 Tbsp.	**Butter**	3 Tbsp.
1 tsp.	**Yeast** *fast rise*	2 tsp.
-or-		
2 tsp.	**Yeast** *active dry*	3 tsp.

Success Hints

• A little icing is a great touch to any of the rolls. We suggest a simple mixture of butter, powdered sugar, and milk drizzled over warm rolls.

• Give your rolls a flavor boost by adding cinnamon to the basic *dough* recipe. (1 1/2 tsp. for a regular loaf and 2 tsp. for a large)

• You can make whole wheat sweet rolls by substituting wheat bread flour for half of the white bread flour and adding 1 tsp. of gluten to a regular loaf and 1 1/2 tsp. to a large.

• Sprinkling crushed nuts on top before baking adds taste and texture.

• Substitute your favorite jams or fillings in these roll recipes.

Peanut Butter Filling

regular		large
1/4 cup	**Butter**	1/3 cup
1/3 cup	**Sugar**	1/2 cup
1/3 cup	**Peanut Butter**	1/2 cup
1/4 cup	**Peanuts** *dry roasted*	1/3 cup

We baked these in an oval glass pan setting them about 1 inch apart before rising. Kids love these. If your kids are big peanut butter and jelly fans, cut the peanut butter in half and make up the measurement with their favorite jelly!

Orange Filling

regular		large
3 Tbsp.	**Butter**	1/4 cup
1/3 cup	**Sugar**	1/2 cup
4 Tbsp.	**Orange Zest** *fresh/grated*	1/3 cup
3 Tbsp.	**Pecans** *chopped*	1/4 cup

* Only use the orange part of orange peel. The white part is bitter.

We placed the rolls in an oval pan about 1 inch apart before the rise. For citrus lovers try frosting with basic frosting mixed with 2 Tbsp. orange zest.

Apple Filling

regular		large
3 Tbsp.	**Butter**	1/4 cup
1/2 cup	**Apple Pie Filling** *canned*	3/4 cup
1/3 cup	**Sugar**	1/2 cup
2 tsp.	**Cinnamon**	1 Tbsp.
3 Tbsp.	**Pecans** *chopped*	1/4 cup

For this filling we like the Strudel Dough Techniques shown on page E-6. We use different fillings for different seasons. Cranberry filling is perfect for holidays.

Raspberry Filling

regular		large
1/4 cup	**Butter**	1/3 cup
1/4 cup	**Raspberry Jam**	1/2 cup
1 tsp.	**Cinnamon**	2 Tbsp.
3 Tbsp.	**Walnuts** *chopped*	1/4 cup

We formed these rolls using the Tea Ring method shown on page E-5 in Dough Techniques. (Remember, you can substitute any jam here you wish.) The Tea Ring is great when you need a fancy pastry but are short on time.

Cherry Filling

regular		large
1/4 cup	**Butter**	1/3 cup
1/2 cup	**Cherry Pie Filling** *canned*	3/4 cup
1/4 cup	**Sugar**	1/3 cup
2 tsp.	**Cinnamon**	1 Tbsp.
3 Tbsp.	**Walnuts** *chopped*	1/4 cup

We baked this recipe by placing individual rolls in jumbo muffin tins to rise. This works great for brunches because it takes the hassle out of cutting and serving the rolls.

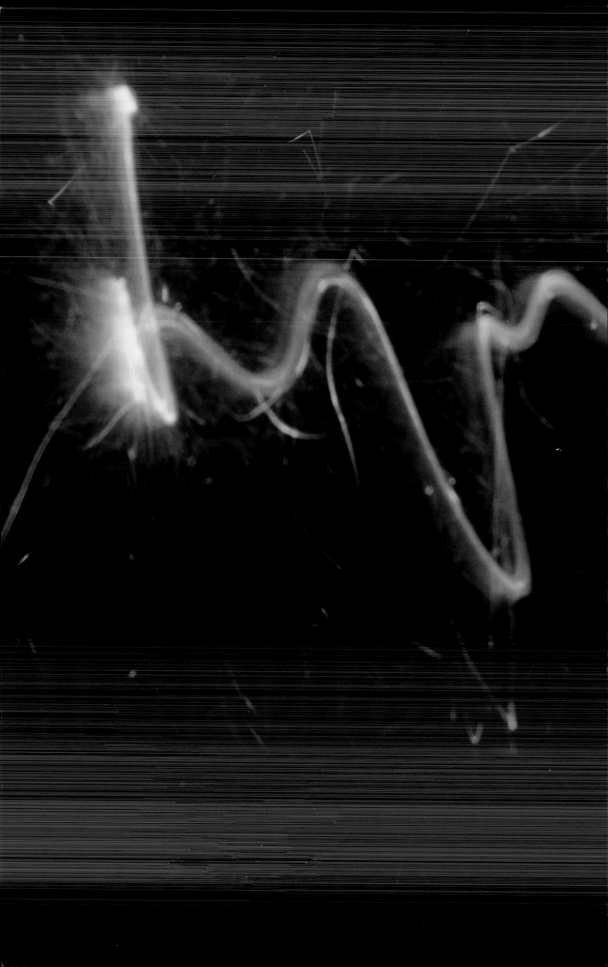

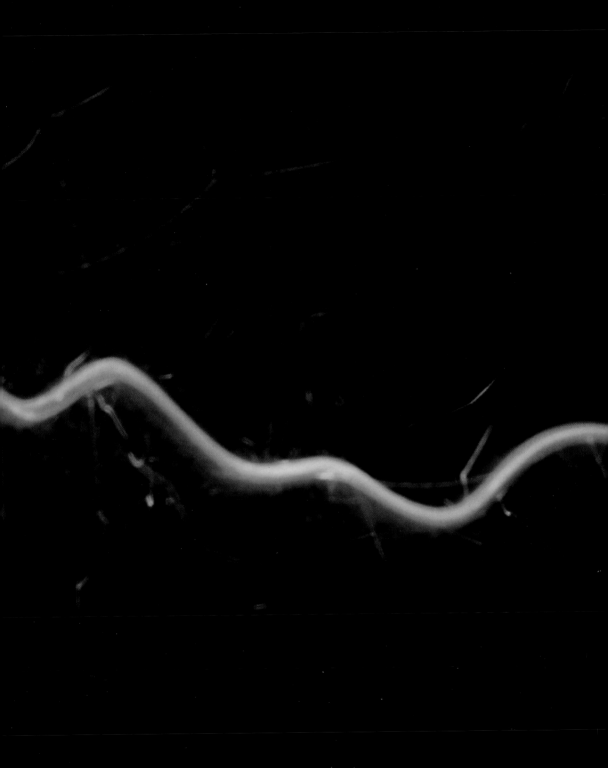

EXTRAS

Dough techniques, the latest in
accessories, and some special surprises!

Dough Techniques

Hamburger Buns

Remove dough to a floured surface. Make 10 balls for a large loaf and 6 for a regular. Place on greased baking sheet and flatten to 1" thickness. (If desired, brush with egg wash and sprinkle with topping.) Let rise until double in size, about 1 hour. Bake at 375° for 15-20 minutes. Brush with butter after baking to insure soft buns.

*Suggested **Electric Bread** recipes:* Garden Herb, Spicy Beef, Onion, Garlic Blues, Saffron and Creamy Rye.

Crescent Rolls

Remove dough to a floured surface. Roll dough into 8" circles, 1/4" thick (2 circles for large and 1 for regular). Cut circles into equal pieces. Roll up wedge starting at widest end. Place on greased baking sheet with point down. Form to make crescent shape and let rise until double in size, about 1 hour. Bake at 375° for 15-20 minutes.

*Suggested **Electric Bread** recipes:* Honey Wheat, Bits o' Bacon, Cheezy Ranch, and Reuben, Reuben.

Basic Loaf

Remove dough to a floured surface. Slowly form into loaf shape, pushing air bubbles out. Place in center of greased loaf pan, 9" x 5" for a large loaf and 8" x 4" for regular. Let rise until about double in size – about 1 hour. Bake at 375° for 15-20 minutes.

*Suggested **Electric Bread** recipes:* Any or all!

Basic Rolls

Remove dough to floured surface. Divide into 12 equal pieces for a large loaf and 8 for a regular. Form into balls and place in a greased baking pan 1/2" apart. Brush rolls with egg wash and sprinkle with seeds if desired. Let rise until double in size, about 1 hour. Bake at 375° for 15-20 minutes until golden brown. (For crusty rolls, bake 1 1/2" apart on a greased baking sheet.)

*Suggested **Electric Bread** recipes:* Zesty Orange, Greek Isle, Creamy Rye, 100% Crunch, Millet and Cottage Dill.

Mini Loaves

Remove dough to a floured surface. Divide into 4 sections for a large loaf and 3 for a regular. Make into balls then slowly form into a sausage shape. Place in greased mini loaf pan and let rise until double in size, about 1 hour. Bake at 375° for 12-17 minutes. If desired brush with egg wash and sprinkle seed topping before rising.

*Suggested **Electric Bread** recipes:* Toasted Onion, Thai, Health Grain, Rice Pudding, and Kulich.

Kaiser Rolls

Remove dough to floured surface. Divide into 12 pieces for a large loaf and 8 for a regular. Flatten into 4" rounds. Pull one edge into center and press down right side. Lift point and bring to center, push right side down again. Repeat step a total of 6 times - pressing hard in center to prevent opening during bak-

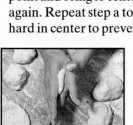

ing. Place on greased baking sheet and let rise until double in size, about 1 hour. Spray with water before baking and place pan of water on bottom shelf of oven during baking. Bake at 375° for 15 – 20 minutes.

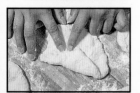   

*Suggested **Electric Bread** recipes:* Classic White, Pepper Corn, Outrageously Oatmeal, Creamy Rye and French Wheat.

Fan Tans

Roll out dough on floured surface into a 9" x 6" rectangle for a large loaf and 6" square for a regular. Brush with butter. Cut dough lengthwise into 1" strips and then stack into piles. Cut stacks into 1" squares. Place on sides in greased muffin tin and let rise until double in size, about 1 hour. Bake at 375° for 15-20 minutes. (For a change of pace, use 2 different bread doughs alternating strips of each dough.)

*Suggested **Electric Bread** recipes:* Whole Wheat Spice, Homestyle White, Tomato Basil, and Zesty Orange.

Pin Wheels

On floured surface, roll dough into a rectangle 1/2" thick and brush with butter. Cut into 3" squares. Make 1 1/2" cut at each corner towards center. Pull corners into center and press down slightly to the right. Place on greased baking sheet, allow to double in size, about 1 hour. Bake at 375° for 15-20 minutes. For a treat, spread dough with pureed pie filling or cream cheese before folding.

*Suggested **Electric Bread** recipes:* Portuguese Sweet, Luscious Luau, Cherry Yogurt, Chocolate, and Almond Poppy.

Twists

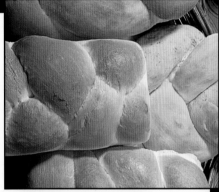

Remove dough to floured surface. Divide in half. Roll each portion into a 1 1/2" sausage shapes. Pinch one end together, cross lengths over each other until you reach the end of the rope, pinch to seal ends. Place in a greased loaf pan or baking sheet, tucking ends under. Let rise until double in size, about 1 hour. Bake at 375° for 20-25 minutes. For a different look, connect ends to form a circle. Twists can be made with one bread or 2 different doughs twisted together, as we've done here.

 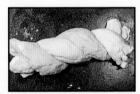 

*Suggested **Electric Bread** recipes:* Homestyle White/Very Berry, Cajun Spice or Tomato Basil/Classic White.

Cloverleaf Rolls

Remove dough to a floured surface. Form into 1/2" balls, 36 for a large loaf and 24 for a regular. Place 3 balls in each greased muffin tin and let rise until double in size, about 1 hour. Bake at 375° for 20-25 minutes. For added interest and flavor, brush with egg wash and sprinkle oats or seeds on top before rise. Or use different bread doughs for each ball to create a decorative party bread.

*Suggested **Electric Bread** recipes:* Garden Herb, Garlic Blues, Multigrain & More, and Irish Soda.

Tea Ring

Remove dough to a floured surface. Roll into 10" x 12" for large loaf and 10" x 10" for regular. Generously spread butter over dough followed by other "wet" ingredients and then sprinkle "dry" ingredients. Roll dough up into log and press seam closed using a drop or two

of water. Form log into a ring on a greased baking sheet & then cut 3/4 way through ring every 1 1/2 inches. Let rise until double in size, about 1 hour. Bake at 375° for 15 to 20 minutes. Fill your Tea Ring with any of the Fillings shown on pages R-13 to R-16.

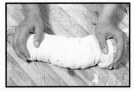

*Suggested **Electric Bread** recipes:* Basic Sweet Roll Dough, Espresso, Smoky Almond, and Sweet Ho Yin.

Bread Sticks

Remove dough to a floured surface. Divide into 18 pieces for a large loaf and 12 for a regular. Roll each piece into a rope aproximately 8" in length. Gently coat with butter on all sides. Roll in seeds - sesame and poppy work great. Bake 1" apart on a greased sheet at 375° for 10-15 minutes until golden brown. For softer bread sticks, place in a greased pan 1/4" apart and let rise.

*Suggested **Electric Bread** recipes:* Cheezy Ranch, Italian Wheat, Onion, Garlic Blues, and Easy French.

Strudel

Place dough on a floured surface. Roll into 10" x 14" for large loaf and 8" x 10" for a regular. Make 2" diagonal cuts up each side of the rectangle. Spread the fruit topping of your choice down the center of rectangle. Lace 2 bottom diagonals over each other to secure end, then from top, lace diagonals over one another until secured at other end. Let rise until double in size, about 1 hour. Bake at 375° for 20-25 minutes.

*Suggested **Electric Bread** recipes:* Basic Sweet Roll, Chocolate, Honey Wheat, Espresso and Classic White.

French Baguettes

Remove dough to a floured surface. Divide into three pieces for a large loaf and two for a regular. Make equal length sausage shaped sections by rolling dough back and forth and pressing. Place on greased French bread pan or baking sheet dusted with cornmeal. Let rise until double in size, about 1 hour. Brush with milk and make 3 long diagonal slashes with a sharp knife or razor blade. Bake at 400° for 25–30 minutes until golden brown.

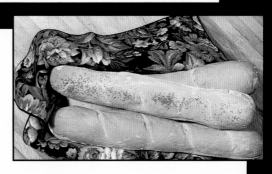

*Suggested **Electric Bread** recipes:* French Wheat, Easy French, Millet and Sourdough White

Gemini Rolls

Place dough onto floured surface. Divide dough into 12 pieces for a large loaf and 8 for a regular. Roll or shape pieces into 3" by 3" squares and brush with butter. Roll up from one side to the center then roll opposing side to center. Place close together in greased baking pan and let rise until double in size - about 1 hour. Bake at 350° for 20-25 minutes. These are great rolls - after baking you can pull open and use for hot dog buns or sandwiches.

*Suggested **Electric Bread** recipes:* Honey Mustard, Italian Wheat, Cinco de Mayo, and Reuben, Reuben.

Accessories

DOUGH KIT - Here are the tools and the toppings you need to turn plain dough into mouth watering bagels and focaccia. Start with a wooden roller to shape the dough, add an easy-to-hold cutter, and a heat-resistant slotted spoon for boiling bagels. We also provide gourmet toppings in these handy 4-spice sprinklers. Bagel topping jar includes sesame seeds, toasted onion, poppy seed and cinnamon sugar. Focaccia jar includes tomato and herb, Italian spice, Italian pepper and spiced cheese.

   Five-piece Dough Kit -$14.95
   Bagel or Focaccia Topper only - $4.00/jar

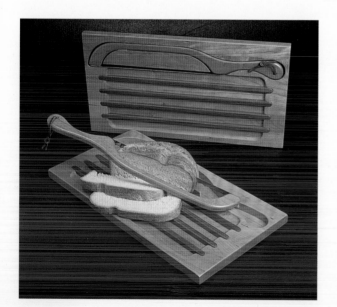

CRUMB BOARD WITH INLAID BOW KNIFE – Designed exclusively for *Electric Bread*®, these sets are handsome enough to put right on your table. Bow knife with carbon steel blade glides through warm bread so you can serve fresh loaves right from the machine! Custom carved of cherry wood with black walnut strips, this American made set makes a perfect gift. $49.95

MORE BOUNTY - These ingredients will stock your kitchen for loaves of fun with *More Electric Bread®*. No need to shop, just start baking. Selection includes wild rice, wheat berry, millet, flax seed, Thai chili paste, instant espresso, garlic paste, taco seasoning, golden raisins, seasoned pepper and a full pound of Berry Medley! All for $44.95.

CUTE COVER-UPS - Why put your machine away when these washable covers can make them part of the decor? Designed to fit all single-loaf machines, choose ivory with green or blue trim; white with black or green trim; or floral.

Solid colors	$20
Floral pattern	$22

NEW WAYS TO MEASURE - If you want to weigh your ingredients like the chefs do – or if you're watching your weight – our handy combination scale and measuring cup is for you. Scale has pounds and kilograms and the 6 1/2 cup measuring cup shows metric measures too. $28

Our new Adjust-A Cup is perfect for measuring messy ingredients like molasses, yogurt, and peanut butter. Set cup to desired measure, fill, level and push the ingredients into the pan. Wow! – $8

BAGEL BITER - Slice your bagel not your fingers with this fool-proof, kid-friendly slicer. Special design makes it impossible for fingers to come in contact with the serrated high carbon stainless steel blade. Simply drop your bagel into the plastic casing, push the handle and you have two perfectly *painless* slices!

White	$34
Walnut	$44

TOOLS FOR TROUBLESOME TASKS

TOOLS FOR TROUBLESOME TASKS - Tired of burning your fingers while fishing toast and bagels out of your toaster? Our wooden toaster tongs are a simple but ingenious solution. • Pesky crumbs are just a memory with our battery-operated table vacuum, the Crumster. It really works! • Does your kneading paddle stick in your loaf? The test kitchen used needle-nosed plyers until we thought of this. One flip of the wrist and our wooden bread hook liberates the paddle without mauling your loaf. • Get the last drop of expensive, concentrated pastes when you use a tube dispenser. Tubes stand upright in your refrigerater, too. $4 each or all four tools for $12.95.

SPACE-SAVING STORAGE - This under-the-cabinet bread box is the perfect solution to kitchen counter overload. Designed in heavy duty, break-resistant white, it holds all loaf sizes with room to spare for bagels and rolls. Fits under any cabinet, flush or recessed. $30.

COZY BREAD KEEPERS - Just the thing for your country kitchen, these washable cotton bags hold any size loaf. They make great gift bags for house warmings. Available in blue, green or black with wooden ring closure. $9.

SIMPLE STORAGE - Here's an inexpensive way to keep your flour fresh and dry. A set of plastic storage bins, perfectly sized for 10 lb. and 5 lb. bags of flour. $12 for the Set.

HEART-OF-THE-KITCHEN ISLAND -
This solid wood cart is large enough to hold your machine and all your baking supplies. Island features both open and covered storage, ample 36" x 20" working surface and an open shelf with access from all four sides. Small shelves on both ends are perfect for storing spices, and the big drawer is a natural home for those odd gadgets. Heavy duty locking casters mean you can move it easily. Assembly required. $299.

SLICING SIMPLICITY - Here are
two simple little gizmos to make life easier. Our beechwood bread slicer produces uniform 1/2" slices for sandwiches and toast every time. The matching bagel slicer is a handy way to ensure safer, even cutting.
Bagel slicer $8.95
Bread slicer $12.95

BERRY MEDLEY - Savor the taste of summer straw-
berries and the tang of autumn cranberries all year long with Chukar brand dried fruits. Featured in our Holiday Cranberry, Cherry Yogurt and Very Berry breads, they transform simple fruit bread into something special. One pound Berry Medley of strawberries, blueberries, and cranberries, $15. Cherries only $11. Cranberries only $8.

**Accessory
Hotline
1-800-541-2733**

Bloomies
Bread and Butter
Catskill Craftsmen, Inc.
ConAgra Grocery Products
Curtis & Campbell
Design Craft, Ltd.
Empak
Frieling USA. Inc.
Giftbox, Inc.
Gourmac, Inc.
Habitat
KitchenArt
Larien Products

Lawry's Foods
Libber
Mad Dog Graphx
Maverick Ventures
Mountain Woods
Norpro
Out of the Woods
Regal Ware
Spice Islands
Stone-Buhr

StyleMasters
The Bakertowne, Inc.
The Computer Store
TimeFrame
Xcell International

Special Thanks

American Harvest
Arrowhead Mills
Bakipan
Betty Crocker - HPA
Black & Decker
Charlescraft
Chukar Cherries
Decosonic
Fleischmann's Yeast
Gold Medal-General Mills
Goldstar
Hitachi
MK Overseas
Mr Coffee
Panasonic Company
Pillsbury
Red Star Yeast
Rogers Flour
SAF Products Corporation
Salton-Maxim
Sanyo-Fisher USA
Sunbeam - Oster
Toastmaster
Welbilt Appliance Company
West Bend
Zojirushi American Corporation

Thanks to Bean's Cafe and
Catholic Social Services for
helping find homes for
16,000 loaves of bread.

Jerry Able
Cindy Alexander
Don Alexander
Virginia Alexander
David Anderson
Pam Auld
Mark Balsalma
Barbara Baugh
Shelly Bender
Steve Bender
Karen Blanchard
Pat Boehm
Red Bradley
Dennis Brandon
Maggie Carey
Dick Carpenter
Shelly Clemins
Jim Dobbelaire
Brian Darcy
Lorelle Delmotto
John Ellenberger

Mary Jo Exley
Boyd Foster
Joanne Frankel
Pamela Fritz
Vicky Gagliano
Steve Goldblatt
Erika Gray
Carl Haggar
Eugene Hanks
Helga Hansen
Jeff Hamano
Bob Hebner
Augusto Hernandez
Evelyn Hull
Linda Jowe
Lou Kahn
Bruce Kiessling
Mary Kiessling
Dave Lackey
Scott Laird
Vern Laird

Anita Lee
Chris Lozzio
Reggie Merchant
Jim MacKay
Beth McKay
John McKay
Cameron McKay
Martin McKay
Jennifer Moody
Ken Normura
Tennys Owens
Al Parrish
Scott Peterson
Julie Phillips
Robert Porter
Dru Renschler
Bernard Schnacke
Monica Schnacke
Bill Sheffield
Terri Skillen

Kate Swalling
Matthew Swalling
Paul Swalling
Ryann Swalling
Bob Tablinsky
Craig Tilly
Laura Tilly
Sam Tilly
Mary Thompson
Brian Thornquist
Eileen Toomey
JoAnn Turchaney
Cheree Vohs
Johnathon Warmund
Dave Weisenberg
Barbara Westfield
Marilyn Wise
Z.J. Loussac Library
Reference Desk

ACKNOWLEDGEMENTS

Test Kitchen Team

Tim Doebler, C.W.C., C.C.E.
Executive Chef

Lynn Brandon

Renie Brandow

Emilia Ponomarev

Carol Rude

Jonell Snook-Holmes

Mary Ann Swalling

JoAnn Wagner

Special Projects

Lara Parrish

Technical Assistance

Colorprint International Co.
Sergei Didyk
Greg Forte, C.E.C., C.C.E.
Helen Ide
Lanrie Leung
Patti McBride
Photowright
Gretchen Sagan

Management

Ann Parrish
Chris Swalling
Shirley Laird

The Recipes of
BREAD ®
electric

Breads:

Almond Poppy, 52
Apple Oat, 42
Apricot, 86
Baked Potato, 76
Banana Granola, 118
Bits o' Bacon, 72
Bleu Cheese & Port, 114
Cajun Spice, 50
Calzone, 124
Carrot, 68
Certainly Citrus, 46
Challah, 82
Cherry Yogurt, 24
Chocolate Cherry, 104
Cinco de Mayo, 22
Classic White, 26
Cottage Dill, 48
100% Crunch, 78
Easy French, 62
Fall Harvest, 106
Fruit Spiral, 130
Garden Herb, 80
Garlic, 56
Greek Isle, 110
Health Grain, 20
Honey Bran English Muffins, 126
Honey Mustard, 40
Honey Wheat, 54
Italian Wheat, 70
Kulich, 36

Light Rye, 64
Luscious Luau, 94
Maraschino Pecan, 60
Mocha Java, 84
Multi-Grain & More, 38
Nutty Coconut, 100
Onion, 90
Orange Kisses, 132
Outrageously Oatmeal, 102
Peaches & Cream, 98
Peanut Butter, 44
Pepper Jack Ties, 136
Picnic Basket, 138
Pizza Pleasure, 96
Pumpernickel, 88
Raisin Bread, 28
Rum Raisin, 92
Saffron, 58
Saffron Braids, 128
Saucy Apple, 74
Sourdough White, 116
Sticky Buns, 134
Sun Nut, 112
Swedish Limpa, 32
Sweet Coconut Curry, 66
Tabouli, 108
Tangy Cranberry, 120
Tropical Medley, 34
100% Whole Wheat, 30

Spread Recipes: 142-143

Brie Walnut, Caraway Blue Cheese, Cheesy Lemon, Chive Roquefort, Curried Butter, Ginger Pecan Butter, Green Peppercorn Butter, Gruyere Apple, Guava-Raisin, Honey Butter, Hot Chili & Garlic Butter, Jezebel Jam, Lemon Mustard Butter, Orange Honey Butter, Paskha, Simple Chutney Cheese, Tarragon-Salmon, Zippy Blue Cheese

The Recipes of
MORE *electric* BREAD®

Breads:

Cheezy Ranch, O43
Chocolate, O49
Cinnamon Sunrise, O1
Corn Fritter, O31
Creamy Rye, O53
Espresso, O9
French Wheat, O17
Garlic Blues, O27
Holiday Cranberry, O39
Home Style White, O47
Irish Soda, O13
Jodi's Rum Cake, O57
Kugelhopf, O23
Maple Walnut, O21
Mexican Sunset, O3
Millet, O15
Olive, O19
Onion Walnut, O33
Pepper Corn, O11
Portuguese Sweet, O59
Reuben, Reuben, O45
Rice Pudding, O29
Smoky Almond, O55
Spicy Beef, O35

Sweet Ho Yin, O51
Thai Bread, O37
Three Seeds, O5
Tomato Basil, O25
Very Berry, O7
Whole Wheat Spice, O63
Wild Rice, O41
Zesty Orange, O61

Bagels:

Basic, R1
Cheese, R4
Cinnamon Raisin, R5
Cranberry Orange, R6
Garlic, R6
Onion, R5
Pumpkin Spice, R4
Whole Wheat, R3

Focaccia:

Ambrosia, R12
Apple, R12
Basic w/Garlic-Herb, R7
Rosemary Cheese, R11
Simple, R11
Sun Dried Tomato, R9
Sweet Pepper, R10
Tomato & Onion, R10

Sweet Rolls:

Apple Filled, R16
Basic Cinnamon Rolls, R13
Cherry Filled, R16
Orange Filled, R16
Peanut Butter Filled, R15
Raspberry Filled, R16

Index

Accessories, E7 to E10

Bagel Recipes, R1 to R6
Basic, R1
Cheese, R4
Cinnamon Raisin, R5
Cranberry Orange, R6
Garlic, R6
Onion, R5
Pumpkin Spice, R4
Whole Wheat, R3

Bread Recipes, O1 to O63
Cheezy Ranch, O43
Chocolate, O49
Cinnamon Sunrise, O1
Corn Fritter, O31
Creamy Rye, O53
Espresso, O9
French Wheat, O17
Garlic Blues, O27
Holiday Cranberry, O39
Home Style White, O47
Irish Soda, O13
Jodi's Rum Cake, O57
Kugelhopf, O23
Maple Walnut, O21
Mexican Sunset, O3
Millet, O15
Olive, O19
Onion Walnut, O33
Pepper Corn, O11
Portuguese Sweet, O59
Reuben, Reuben, O45
Rice Pudding, O29
Smoky Almond, O55
Spicy Beef, O35
Sweet Ho Yin, O51
Thai Bread, O37
Three Seeds, O5
Tomato Basil, O25
Very Berry, O7
Whole Wheat Spice, O63
Wild Rice, O41
Zesty Orange, O61

Dough Techniques, E1 to E6
Basic Loaf
Basic Rolls
Bread Sticks
Cloverleaf Rolls
Crescent Rolls
Fan Tans
French Baguettes
Gemini Rolls
Hamburger Buns
Kaiser Rolls
Mini Loaves
Pin Wheels
Strudel
Tea Ring
Twists

Focaccia Recipes, R7 to R12
Ambrosia, R12
Apple, R12
Basic w/Garlic-Herb, R7
Rosemary Cheese, R11
Simple, R11
Sun Dried Tomato, R9
Sweet Pepper, R10
Tomato & Onion, R10

Manufacturers - Bread Machines, M1

Only by Machine, O1 to O63

Quick Reminders, M3 to M4
Eggs
Extra Knead
Fruit
Loading Your Machine
Measuring
Only By Machine
Recipe Size
Spoilage
Water Temperature

Rolled and Pulled, R1 to R16

Sweet Roll Recipes, R13 to R16
Apple Filled
Basic Cinnamon Rolls
Cherry Filled
Orange Filled
Peanut Butter Filled
Raspberry Filled

Bread Name

regular   large
_____

_____   **Water**   _____

_____   **White Flour**   _____

_____   **Wheat Flour**   _____

_____   **Dry Milk**   _____

_____   **Sugar**   _____

_____   **Salt**   _____

_____   **Butter**   _____

                             Other Ingredients:

_____   _____   _____

_____   _____   _____

_____   _____   _____

_____   _____   _____

_____   _____   _____

_____   **Yeast**   _____
                                    fast rise

_____   **Yeast**   _____
                                    active dry

Use this page to formulate your own new breads. If you want to share, mail or fax a copy to:
Innovative Cooking Enterprises, I.C.E. • P.O. Box 240888 • Anchorage, Alaska 99524-0888
Fax - (907) 561-1835

Bread Name

regular　　　　　　　　　　　　　　　　　large

_____　　　　**Water**　　　　_____

_____　　**White Flour**　　_____

_____　　**Wheat Flour**　　_____

　　　　　　　　　Dry Milk

_____　　　　**Sugar**　　　_____

　　　　　　　　　　Salt

_____　　　　**Butter**　　　_____

Other Ingredients:

_____　　_____　　_____

_____　　_____　　_____

_____　　_____　　_____

_____　　_____　　_____

_____　　_____　　_____

_____　　　**Yeast**　　　_____
　　　　　　　　　fast rise

_____　　　**Yeast**　　　_____
　　　　　　　　　active dry

Use this page to formulate your own new breads. If you want to share, mail or fax a copy to:
Innovative Cooking Enterprises, I.C.E. • P.O. Box 240888 • Anchorage, Alaska 99524-0888
Fax - (907) 561-1835

Bread Name

regular   **large**

_____   Water   _____

_____   White Flour   _____

_____   Wheat Flour   _____

_____   Dry Milk   _____

_____   Sugar   _____

_____   Salt   _____

_____   Butter   _____

Other Ingredients:

_____   _____   _____

_____   _____   _____

_____   _____   _____

_____   _____   _____

_____   _____   _____

_____   **Yeast**   _____
                       fast rise

_____   **Yeast**   _____
                       active dry

Use this page to formulate your own new breads. If you want to share, mail or fax a copy to:
Innovative Cooking Enterprises, I.C.E. • P.O. Box 240888 • Anchorage, Alaska 99524-0888
Fax - (907) 561-1835

Bread Name

regular		large
_____	**Water**	_____
_____	**White Flour**	_____
_____	**Wheat Flour**	_____
_____	**Dry Milk**	_____
_____	**Sugar**	_____
_____	**Salt**	_____
_____	**Butter**	_____

Other Ingredients:

regular		large
_____	_____	_____
_____	_____	_____
_____	_____	_____
_____	_____	_____
_____	_____	_____

_____	**Yeast** *fast rise*	_____
_____	**Yeast** *active dry*	_____

Use this page to formulate your own new breads. If you want to share, mail or fax a copy to:
Innovative Cooking Enterprises, I.C.E. • P.O. Box 240888 • Anchorage, Alaska 99524-0888
Fax - (907) 561-1835

Bread Name

regular   **large**

_____   Water   _____

_____   White Flour   _____

_____   Wheat Flour   _____

                   Dry Milk

                   Sugar

_____   Salt   _____

_____   Butter   _____

Other Ingredients:

_____   _____   _____

_____   _____   _____

_____   _____   _____

_____   _____   _____

_____   _____   _____

_____   **Yeast**   _____
                   fast rise

                   Yeast
_____   _active dry_   _____

Use this page to formulate your own new breads. If you want to share, mail or fax a copy to:
Innovative Cooking Enterprises, I.C.E. • P.O. Box 240888 • Anchorage, Alaska 99524-0888
Fax - (907) 561-1835

Bread Name

regular   large

_____   **Water**   _____

_____   **White Flour**   _____

_____   **Wheat Flour**   _____

_____   **Dry Milk**   _____

_____   **Sugar**   _____

_____   **Salt**   _____

_____   **Butter**   _____

Other Ingredients:

_____   _____   _____

_____   _____   _____

_____   _____   _____

_____   _____   _____

_____   _____   _____

_____   _____   _____

_____   **Yeast**   _____
fast rise

_____   **Yeast**   _____
active dry

Use this page to formulate your own new breads. If you want to share, mail or fax a copy to:
Innovative Cooking Enterprises, I.C.E. • P.O. Box 240888 • Anchorage, Alaska 99524-0888
Fax - (907) 561-1835

— Bread Name —

regular   **large**

_____   **Water**   _____

_____   **White Flour**   _____

_____   **Wheat Flour**   _____

_____   **Dry Milk**   _____

_____   **Sugar**   _____

_____   **Salt**   _____

_____   **Butter**   _____

Other Ingredients:

_____ _____ _____

_____ _____ _____

_____ _____ _____

_____ _____ _____

_____ _____ _____

_____ _____ _____

_____   **Yeast**   _____
fast rise

_____   **Yeast**   _____
active dry

Use this page to formulate your own new breads. If you want to share, mail or fax a copy to:
Innovative Cooking Enterprises, I.C.E. • P.O. Box 240888 • Anchorage, Alaska 99524-0888
Fax - (907) 561-1835

Bread Name

regular   large

_____	Water	_____
_____	White Flour	_____
_____	Wheat Flour	_____
_____	Dry Milk	_____
_____	Sugar	_____
_____	Salt	_____
_____	Butter	_____

Other Ingredients:

_____   _____   _____

_____   _____   _____

_____   _____   _____

_____   _____   _____

_____   _____   _____

_____   **Yeast**   _____
fast rise

_____   **Yeast**   _____
active dry

Use this page to formulate your own new breads. If you want to share, mail or fax a copy to:
Innovative Cooking Enterprises, I.C.E. • P.O. Box 240888 • Anchorage, Alaska 99524-0888
Fax - (907) 561-1835